THE UPSTART GUIDE TO

OWNING AND MANAGING AN ANTIQUES BUSINESS

THE UPSTART GUIDE TO
OWNING AND MANAGING AN ANTIQUES BUSINESS

Lisa Angowski Rogak

UPSTART PUBLISHING COMPANY, INC.
The Small Business Publishing Company
Dover, New Hampshire

Published by Upstart Publishing Company, Inc.
A Division of Dearborn Publishing Group, Inc.
12 Portland Street
Dover, New Hampshire 03820
(800) 235-8866 or (603) 749-5071

Neither the author nor the publisher of this book is engaged in rendering, by the
sale of this book, legal, accounting or other professional services. The reader is
encouraged to employ the services of a competent professional in such matters.

Library of Congress Cataloging-in-Publication Data
Rogak, Lisa Angowski.
    The upstart guide to owning and managing an antiques business /
Lisa Angowski Rogak.
        p.   cm.
    Includes index.
    ISBN: 0-936894-66-0
        1. Secondhand trade—United States. 2. Selling—Antiques—United
States. 3. New business enterprises—United States. I. Title.
    HF5482.R64 1995
    745.1'068—dc20   94-31492
                                                                     CIP

Cover design by Paul Perlow Design, New York, NY.
Back cover photo by David Parker.

Printed in the United States of America
10 9 8 7 6 5 4 3 2 1

For a complete catalog of Upstart's small business publications, call (800) 235-8866.

For Dan

CONTENTS

PREFACE

I am not normally what you would call a *thing* person. My heart doesn't palpitate in gift shops or hardware stores, and my friends and family always puzzle over what to get me for birthdays and holidays. "You're so hard to shop for," they lament. "You don't have anything, and you don't want anything, either."

Up until now, that is. In researching and writing this book, I collected more than 50 of the newspapers and magazines devoted to the art of buying and selling antiques and collectibles. Most include features that spotlight one particular item that's currently in favor among collectors. The thousands of ads I scanned sometimes made my eyes hurt:

Wanted: Assorted Ephemera. I Buy Bye-lo Dolls, Any Condition. For Sale: Sterling Silver Mustache Cups.

At times, it got a little strange:

I Buy Safety Razors & Their Instructions. Wanted: Shrunken Heads, Ethnicity Not Important.

The list goes on—Antique dental tools, old candy wrappers, Chatty Cathy dolls, Nazi daggers, pencil sharpener souvenirs shaped like the Empire State Building.

But I must admit that here and there were a few items that caught my eye that others, in all likelihood, will probably label strange: children's pedal cars, teddy bears that were manufactured when their original namesake—Teddy Roosevelt—

occupied the White House, and a rare doll of the cereal cartoon character Quake from the Seventies that was mine (back then) for three box tops and a dollar, but which runs to almost $200 today. Though some people might label some of my interests as non-antiques, I've learned that no matter what you collect, and no matter how obscure an object, you'll be able to find somebody who collects it *and* someone who will pay you good money for it.

And so this book stretches the traditional definition of the word antiques from its original meaning of anything that is at least 100 years old to an object that is considered to be collectible and which wasn't made today. It could rightfully have been manufactured only yesterday, however. In the summer of 1994, characters and collectibles from the movie *The Nightmare before Christmas*, released in November of 1993, already were being advertised in the antiques and collectibles publications with asking prices higher than the original retail.

This is only one example of the reasons why people want to enter the antiques business: the chance to make a quick buck, which is more elusive than you'd realize.

The Upstart Guide to Owning and Managing an Antiques Business will provide you with a crash course in everything you need to know to open your own shop, mall booth, or show exhibit. An antiques business is a dream business for many, but like many dream businesses, there's a lot of hard work behind the scenes that you don't see if you're on this side of the business.

Keep in mind, however, the good side of the antiques business: it will let you collect to your heart's content. And maybe you'll even end up keeping some of your favorite items, instead of letting them go to others.

OPPORTUNITIES

Many people admit that they got into the antiques business because they had accumulated too much stuff and had to get rid of some (allowing them to buy even more). You'll find the field crammed with people who have decided to turn their hobbies into bona fide businesses; you may even find yourself in this category. But even though you may have been collecting for years—whether it's furniture, dolls, or art—you'll quickly find out that it's a whole new ballgame once it's a business. In fact, your greatest gift may be that you are able to spot a fake piece of Fiestaware at 100 paces, but your inexperience means that you're going to get burned—even the pros get burned in this business at times. You may get carried away at an auction and buy an item at a price so high that it will take years to realize a profit on it; you may fall in love with a Victorian fainting couch and believe your customers will do the same—and they don't. Instead, it sits in your inventory, and sits, and sits. You get tired of looking at it and bring it to an auction in the next town just so you never have to see it again, and it fetches a mere 10 percent of what you paid—minus, of course, the auctioneer's commission.

You should also keep in mind that it's likely that in running your antiques business, you will be in touch with people who deal in your particular specialty—World War II binoculars, for instance—yet still dabble in more than one area like you do. The fact is that any person who makes a living from antiques is a goldmine of contacts to help you build your inventory. Competition is not a mainstay of the antiques business, because sooner or later you'll probably end up doing business with everyone in the business you know. And since so many people have discovered that you have to specialize to be successful, if a shopkeeper knows you specialize in Disney movie posters, he'll know to be on the lookout for Disneyana when he's out scouting Shaker furniture for his own shop. He'll probably buy it with the intention of selling it to you for a small profit when he gets home. You'll do the same for him when you're on the road.

This unpredictability is what makes the antiques business so exciting. Bear in mind that even though mistakes will be part of the business, so will the joys of discovering a seemingly run-of-the-mill plate at a yard sale that turns out to be a rare piece of spongeware you can sell for a couple of hundred dollars just a few weeks later.

Your Place in the Business

An antiques business is one business that can be successful in many different forms and on many different levels. You can do it part time or full time, work out of your home, in a shop, or spend most of your time on the road.

You have many more options than to tie yourself down to a shop, although this is the avenue that many prospective antiques entrepreneurs initially choose. Once you discover the infinite variety of selling venues for men and women who enter this business, you will select the one that provides the best fit for your needs and lifestyles. And even though you may opt for a shop, you can use it as your home base so that you can add other offshoots to your business, like exhibiting at shows and flea markets, selling items through the mail, and even offering your appraisal services.

Depending upon which avenues you choose, you'll also be dealing with many different kinds of people, some in person and others you may never meet face to face.

You want to be in the antiques business, so you'll be seeing items that vary in quality and quantity. Whatever you choose, you will be in the business of buying antiques and collectibles to sell them at a profit.

Antiques Shop

When people talk about going into the antiques business, they frequently say they want to open a shop of their own. Owning and operating an antiques shop certainly will provide you with a local and regional reputation and a certain amount of exposure; this is important because people will come to you to buy and sell antiques and collectibles. However, even before your first day of business, you'll already be paying overhead, hiring staff if you don't want to be tied to the store, and spending to advertise and promote the store. Though many people decide to open their shops in a barn or garage on their property, running an antiques shop is still a substantial commitment. Even if you're in the northern half of the country and choose to close up an unheated outbuilding for the winter, off months are a great time to scout around looking for more inventory for next year.

Antiques shops are found everywhere from high-rent, high-traffic urban areas to sleepy rural areas a few miles down a meandering dirt road. The advantage of a shop is a presence in the community as well as a place to recruit new customers outside the regular ones that frequent antique circles.

The drawbacks include the overhead you'll pay to keep the shop open, which is especially disheartening during the slow times of the year, and if you choose to be open year-round and can't afford the expense of hiring help, you'll miss out on the buying opportunities—auctions, flea markets, shows, and just wandering around.

Some people simply don't have the money to invest in either a shop or the inventory to fill it, at least when they're first starting out, and so they choose one or more of the other options available.

Antiques Mall Booth

Running a mall booth antiques business is quickly becoming the fastest growing field in the antiques business. As of 1994 there were several hundred antiques malls in operation across the country, with more being added every week. An antiques mall is a large building or hall where the landlord or manager rents booths, tables, or locked display cases to people who want to exhibit their antiques for sale. Antiques malls are typically in high-traffic areas frequented by tourists. For shoppers, an antiques mall contains many more items than they could ever find in one shop, even a large one. The disadvantage is that each booth contains only a limited amount of merchandise, usually not the cream of the crop, since theft is common at cavernous antiques malls with little or no supervision (one of the disadvantages for the dealer).

However, because of the high traffic, a dealer can hope to turn over merchandise that much quicker. Plus you don't have to be in the mall full-time; most mall exhibitors spend only a couple of hours a month replenishing and rearranging stock. In fact, many people rent space in more than one mall within a region as a way to cover different markets and to test what pulls best at a given location.

It's also relatively inexpensive to get into the business: Booth rentals can range from $40 a month up to $300 or more. Some mall owners will give a discount if you rent more than one booth. Turnover of dealers can be high at an antiques mall, since some test a space for only a few months, and without enough business, they'll pull out. Some malls require you to sign a year's lease, while others offer a month-to-month or even a week-to-week arrangement. Malls may charge you a percentage of each sale in lieu of rent, but most dealers advise against this, as the amount typically turns out to be much more than what a traditional rental would cost.

The management at an antiques mall will keep track of your monthly sales and then send you a check once a month. All you have to do is to restock your booth. The mall collects all money, keeps track of it via coded price tags, and sends a check, some minus the monthly rent, others bill your directly for it.

Unless you're in ten or more antiques malls, you're not likely to make a living from the business, but it's a good way to learn the ropes without a large investment.

Antiques Show Exhibitor

No matter where you are in the United States, regardless of the time of year, the chances are that you won't find it too difficult to locate an antiques show where you can display your wares—or buy from others to replenish your stock.

Antiques shows are frequently held in schools, community halls, churches, elegant hotel ballrooms, large indoor shopping malls, or outdoors in parking lots. This last venue is more likely to be referred to as a flea market than an antiques show, but no matter its name, all of them have some things in common.

Exhibitors pay a fee to participate in the show. A show promoter finds exhibitors—many will travel for hours to get to a show—and also attracts prospective customers, who may or may not pay an admission fee. A few shows are wholesale and open only to dealers who can produce a business card and a tax ID number. Some shows offer "dealers' hours," allowing dealers first pick of the lots.

If you decide to sell your antiques primarily at shows, you will, in essence, be operating an antiques shop on wheels. You will have to set up and break down your merchandise at the end of each show, which typically lasts for three or four days.

With antiques shows, you will be dealing with many more people in one weekend than would probably come into a traditional antiques shop in the course of one year. If you decide to go this route, you will have to be much more of a people person than you would in a stationary shop, since you will be talking with customers pretty much nonstop the entire show. That's why it's best if you can work a show with a partner. Antiques shows can be exhausting. Add to that the stress of travel and living on the road and you'll realize the need to be in good shape and have high stamina.

Most shows charge anywhere from a couple hundred dollars for a booth rental for the weekend up to several thousand dollars. Some show promoters are highly selective about the exhibitors they allow the privilege of renting a booth.

But it's usually worth it. Not only will you sell your merchandise to people who visit the show, but you can have the opportunity to roam the floor and buy from other dealers and they from you. You can also make contacts with other dealers for networking and camaraderie.

Before you invest time and money traveling to a particular show, you should ask other dealers who have exhibited there about their experiences and whether they thought it was worth it. You can also read back issues of *Maine Antiques Digest* and some other publications for honest reports on show attendance figures, the quality of the merchandise, and buying patterns. All this changes from year to year, however. You won't make money on every show, but you can make contacts and draw on that experience for future shows.

Mail Order

Selling your antiques through the mail can be lucrative. However, some antiques specialties are more suitable to this method than others. Books and ephemera (antique paper items, i.e., postcards, old ads, etc.), coins, and other small pieces of collectibles generally do well; these items have a market that is already accustomed to buying and trading through the mail and no special packing or shipping is necessary. This can truly be a kitchen-table business.

Unlike other forms of antiques businesses, however, the sales may not be immediate. Most mail-order antiques dealers get started by placing a small display or classified ad in appropriate publications. Depending upon how the ad is worded and where it is placed, you may be flooded with responses or your mail carrier may get bored. Another way to start your business is to exhibit your merchandise at antiques shows, collect names for your mailing list, and create a brochure marketing other items you left at home. Then, as you build your list, you can mail announcements to your list, alerting your customers to your recent acquisitions.

Building an antiques-by-mail business makes sense if you offer items that are not readily available and if you specialize. Mail order customers are among the most loyal customers around if you have a good list. You can start now to build this business for steady returns over the years.

Private Sales

Like mail order, offering antiques through private sales to individuals and businesses can be lucrative and offer steady income. However, there are a couple of major differences. The items are usually high-ticket items, like rare furniture and clocks, and are expensive to ship and insure. So you'll have to find a way to deliver the goods to your buyer.

If you concentrate on private sales you'll place ads in the major publications, but more to build a reputation and client list than for direct sales. Again, it's almost imperative that you specialize—you'll be dealing with many people who will use you as a search service. The more you know a particular subject, the more calls you will get from potential customers.

They will assume that you will be able to locate an extremely rare item for them. Then you put your feelers out through the network of contacts you have built. Your customers understand that the search will take some time; but they also trust in your ability to get the job done because you've come through for them before.

When dealers find items they know one of their customers will like, they let the customer see it in person, since a phone conversation or even pictures cannot do it justice. Antiques dealers who focus on private sales have to be risk-takers, but if they're good, the eventual pay off is there.

If you love the freelance life and you love to travel, then these last two categories are for you.

Picker

A picker is a devotee of the fast turnaround. A picker usually does just that—picks through other people's treasures in order to sell the finds to dealers, shopkeepers, and others. Pickers tend to concentrate in one specific geographic area. They work on building up their contacts of people to pick from and dealers to sell to, but they also attend a fair share of auctions and antiques shows. Many people are pickers in their spare time. Their primary occupation may involve a significant amount of travel, so they pick as they go. They can also take advantage of the fact that certain items are more popular— and thus more expensive—in one area of the country than another. For instance, there's not much demand for antique Navajo turquoise jewelry in Maine, so a picker can usually buy a sack of rings and necklaces in the Pine Tree State for a song. Two weeks later, off to the Southwest on business, the picker can go into any antiques shop in the area and make back the investment several times over.

Pickers also tend to specialize and work with a limited number of dealers whose needs they're familiar with and can easily fulfill.

Pickers usually sell their finds in the same area they found them, which necessitates only a small pickup or even just a backpack.

Pickers may study the want ads in the various antique trade publications as well as the who-buys-what books like, *Maloney's Antiques & Collectibles Resource Directory* and *Where to Sell It*, and deal exclusively through the mail. In this case, they need not necessarily specialize in one area.

From the dealer's perspective, it's great to sell to pickers. If you have what they want, you'll be able to unload it with no problems. However, this instant cash has its price. You'll probably make less money selling to a picker than at a mall or in a shop on consignment.

Hauler

A hauler is a picker who searches for items in higher volumes, tending to buy in a low-demand area and sell where their purchases are popular.

How do they do it? Often, a hauler must make a number of cross-country buying trips each year. Hauling also requires the use of a large truck, especially if you're going to be dealing in furniture and other large antiques. Some haulers pack and ship their finds back home so they can remain footloose until they run out of auctions or flea markets, which may mean that they stay on the road for months.

In order to make hauling most profitable, it's important to drive a full truck in both directions. That means filling up on items in demand for people in areas you'll be passing through, as well as your final destination—if you have one. And remember the rule of buy low, sell high. It's important that you spend weeks, even months, scouting out your area or weeding out your stockpile of stored antiques and collectibles for those objects that will be easy to unload on the other end of your trip.

Some dealers and others at your home base might ask you to bring some of their items with you on your trip to sell on consignment, but I'd recommend you stay away from making arrangements of this kind. First of all, your share of the sale may be less than half the price. In addition, if you are unable to sell it on your trip, you'll have to lug it back home—it may take up valuable space.

Though pickers concentrate on items that can be sold as soon as possible, haulers may pick up some items that need refinishing or repair before they can be resold. Naturally, this will increase the profit margin, especially if the hauler does the work. Also, the work can be done in the winter when cross-country hauling is not feasible.

Many haulers make an average of 10 to 20 trips a year. Your overhead, which consists of the cost of the truck, insurance, gas, food, and lodging—if you don't sleep in your truck, that is—can add up quickly. Most dealers recommend that only people with a good eye for value and an excellent bargaining ability think about entering the hauling business. Though it can be fun, you'll have to pay no more than 50 percent of what you believe you can sell an item for back home so that you can still make a profit. It's tough to live more than half the year on the road, but if you like to travel and have an eye for antiques, then give it a shot.

Other Possibilities

Appraisers, restorers and repairers, and auctioneers are also possibilities to pursue if you're interested in the antiques business. Each requires special skills and, in the case of appraisers and auctioneers, special courses, seminars, and licensure by the state. These are more services than pure buying and selling opportunities and most people who do enter one of these specialties typically have years of experience in buying and selling antiques.

In the course of running your business you will undoubtedly make contact with appraisers, restorers, and auctioneers, so if you're still interested in pursuing one of these fields later on you will have a ready network.

Current Business Environment

Take a look at the specialized publications for the antiques trade the next time you're at a bookstore or magazine stand. *Art & Antiques, The Magazine Antiques, Treasure Chest, Maine Antique Digest,* the list doesn't seem to stop. Over in the book section on antiques, you'll find beautiful four-color books on almost every category of antique, from Victorian dolls to weathervanes; yes, even some cookie jars and old farm tools. It seems that in the summertime, in almost every city and rural village, an antiques show or auction is being held. At some of the more highly elite antiques shows, you and your items have to be judged to gain the privilege of renting a booth. Most shows are not this exclusive, however, and will rent space to anyone with the booth fee, although that means items in these shows can have a hodgepodge of quality.

This presents a pertinent question: What exactly is an antique, anyway? Purists interpret the term to mean any item that is more than one hundred years old, although judging from the outrageous prices that rusty Tonka trucks circa 1965 and even *Star Wars* and "Charlie's Angels" memorabilia can fetch, an antique can sometimes mean anything that you didn't buy off the shelf today. If you bought it yesterday, it just might be acceptable.

This broad interpretation means there are a lot of people getting into the business because they see how much money they can make from just cleaning out the attic, not for any great love or appreciation for a particular kind of item. You can usually recognize these people at a show or sale; they can't tell you much about an item beyond its price tag or the year it was made. For these people, the antiques business is only one in a long string of get-rich-quick schemes and their numbers swell the ranks of antiques dealers so that the business may seem more competitive than it really is.

In contrast, people in the business because they love antiques are easy to spot: they'll think nothing of spending hours talking with you about their particular line or specialty, rhapsodizing over its attributes and asking detailed questions about similar objects in your collection. Their enthusiasm is all over their faces. Those who are in it for the long haul will profit the most.

There are no hard numbers about how many people are in the business, since so many dabble in it part-time or take a hiatus while they're building their collections up. I've heard that there are 125,000 appraisers in the United States. The number of people who sell antiques and collectibles—whether they work full- or part-time—must be many times that. Most regional antiques newspapers put their readership at an average of 30,000.

The dollar amount estimated to be spent each year on antiques is daunting. As for auction business, a Gallup poll in 1994 stated that $161.7 billion of property was sold at auction in 1992. The pollsters estimate that $70.45 billion figure is livestock and what they deem to be "personal property," which is everything except livestock and cars sold by dealers. Though experts dispute that figure, even half of that number constitutes huge volume since the majority of items at antiques auctions are sold for less than $200.

The volatility of the prices of some antiques lead you to believe that the return on your investment will be infinitely better than in the stock market, especially when you hear stories about the unrestored oil painting by a deaf-mute man from Portland, Maine, in the early 19th century that sold for $68,200 at an auction in the spring of 1994. Unfortunately, one side effect of the great numbers of people in the business is that every time an item is sold, it's marked up in order to earn a profit for its owner. Every year that passes means there are fewer items to be sold from a certain period of time, which only increases the value of the others that remain. For example, a Hoosier cabinet sold for $350 in 1985; today you can't usually find one in good condition for under $1,200, at least on the East Coast and the Midwest where they're most popular.

That's why many in the business develop a specialty in a particular item or historical period—or keep an eye constantly peeled for what will be the next hot item.

And, unlike many businesses where some time and elbow grease will raise your price, the antiques business generally doesn't follow these rules. For instance, if you repair the dents and repaint that beatup Tonka truck you will have lost up to 80 percent of its value. Surprisingly enough, if you leave an item alone, it's entirely possible that it will gain 1,000 percent in value or even more in one day. It doesn't happen often, but it does occur often enough to keep people poking in musty shops, odd lots at auctions, and garage sales that initially appear to be just a jumble of exercise equipment and chipped Corningware.

Future Business Potential

The items produced today will be the antiques of tomorrow, though you may be long gone before their value goes up significantly. And even though most lovers of antiques are packrats, you'd almost have to have a warehouse in order to store everything that might be valuable in another ten or twenty years. Look at all of the memorabilia from the 1970s, like mood rings and lava lamps, that are commanding high prices in the mid-1990s. Back then, who would have thought to hang onto them?

But most people are not choosing the save-everything route. A combination of a good eye, talent for picking quality items in a specific category, and shrewd bargaining will all help to create what holds the key to developing your future business potential—your reputation among the people with whom you do business.

As with any business, if you make the customers happy, they will return. And they'll also refer other buyers to you. Hucksters and people in it for a quick buck usually don't hang around long—they have little repeat business.

Some people start out in the business just selling a few items from their collections at flea markets on weekends and graduate to a few larger shows, attending an auction or two each week and placing an ad in the local paper looking for items. The antiques business is manageable because you can remain small or grow into a thriving business with several employees and a storefront. The business is flexible enough that it's entirely possible to switch between several different levels of the business several times a week—or emphasize a different specialty each year. It's up to you and your desires and goals.

The Antiques Lifestyle

As I've mentioned, most people get into the antiques business because they love and appreciate things, particularly things that are old and have some intrinsic value. Some start out as collectors and in going to antiques shows, shops, and flea markets, they meet a lot of people in the business and think, "It looks like they're having a good time and making some money; maybe *I* can do this, too."

A seed is planted, as well as an obsession. If you choose to enter the business part time at first, you can devote your time to searching for antiques and learning about the best ways to sell them. Perhaps you'll start out by holding an antiques sale in your garage every weekend and placing ads in the newspapers under garage sales. You might then graduate to renting space at an antiques mall and a few regional shows each year. It's a pleasant pastime. Your profits allow you to buy items you never thought you could afford—"Of course it's for sale," you wink, though you hope no one buys it. And you're exposed to many more antiques than if it just remained a hobby.

For some people, this is sufficient. For others, however, it just scratches the surface and they begin to dream of their own shop, a large client list, and acceptance into elite shows. If you fall into this category, you'll see the signs: You'll find that you're on the road any weekend there's a major show within 500 miles; you'll place an ad in one of the major antiques trade publications to announce that you're officially forming your business; then, you'll take another big step and put an ad in your local daily or weekly newspaper, letting the public know that you are actively buying antiques.

Whether you initially choose to work on your business part time or full time, when it comes right down to it, they are really both sides of the same coin. Living a life centered around the buying and selling of antiques means that you are constantly exposed to the past. For people who aren't crazy about either the present or the future, this is certainly one of the big appeals of the business.

For you, a quiet drive in the country simply cannot go uninterrupted, no matter what field of antiques you decide to enter. You'll drive down roads you never knew existed, because whenever you see a sign that says Yard Sale or Tag Sale, you'll have to stop and sift through the offerings, even if it all seems like junk on the surface. "Business, you know," you'll explain to a long-suffering companion. But it *is* justified. The annals of the antiques business are filled with the stories of dealers who made tens of thousands of dollars on some tarnished trinket or bauble they found at the bottom of a 25-cent box at a yard sale. So even though you will be exposed to more worthless junk than priceless items, the chance that you could get lucky lurks at every lowly garage sale.

Income and Profit Potentials

It's believed that the average antique will pass through the hands of seven or eight dealers before it ends up in a private collection. That explains the big markup on a lot of pieces and is the major reason why prices have soared since the late 1980s.

Even though dealers near the end of the chain do make money, the higher the price of an object recently selling for much less means, in many cases, it will take that much longer to make your money back and to make a profit.

So if you want to stand a chance of making a living, buy lower on the antiques food chain.

The potential income antiques dealers can make depends on many factors: yearly volume, the quality and type of their antiques, the number of shows at which they exhibit, their variety of services, how aggressive they are, and how much time they spend on the business. It's possible for part timers to make more than full timers, depending upon the kind and level of antiques they're dealing with. It's safe to say that even if you choose to run your antiques business part time, in actuality, it will turn out closer to full time when you factor in the leisurely country drives searching for antiques, as well as all the time you spend thinking about it and planning for future shows and endeavors.

Again, figures vary, but if you run a strictly weekend operation, exhibiting at shows in season with maybe a booth at an antiques mall or two, it's possible to clear anywhere from $5,000 to $30,000 or more after all of your expenses.

The income of full timers is a little harder to project, since most have more than one type of antiques business—perhaps a shop and private sales business, combined with some mail order and a couple major shows a year. Depending upon the area of the country, the types of antiques you deal in, your clientele, and your overhead, it's possible to gross over a million dollars a year, though many of these multifaceted shops are run by one or two people with some fill-in help as needed. For a full time operation, the range of gross revenue can range from $50,000 to $250,000 a year, though even a shop that's open seasonally can gross $25,000 or $30,000 a year or more, up 30 to 50 percent of which will pay your salary, leaving profit.

Many people in the business part time find the money to be incidental. In fact, I've been told that a large number of people who run a part-time antiques business are only in it to feed their buying habits and usually have a well-paid spouse who also, in essence, is supporting their habit.

This type of antiques business owner never takes the few extra steps necessary to consider their business a full-fledged operation, rather than just a hobby that brings in some money from time to time. Though your eye for antiques must come first, even if your business experience is nil, you can still expect to make a better living if you run your operation like a business. That, by itself, will set you apart from the rest of the people who are in it only for the fun. When other buyers and dealers see how serious you are and that you're in it for the long haul, your business and reputation will only grow, along with your bottom line.

By picking up this book, you've taken a first important step to distinguish yourself as a serious business owner and not just somebody who dabbles in the field.

Risk Potentials

Going into any business, not just an antiques business, is fraught with risk—especially a business where purchases frequently are made on emotion and not investment possibilities. You have a ready-made situation where the prices of your inventory can rise and fall, then rise again quite rapidly, all in the course of a few hours.

Even seasoned pros who have dealt in antiques for 20 or more years will admit that theirs is a risky business. You never know for sure if a buyer will want that Revolutionary War era chest that you spent three years and 1,500 miles tracking down. If she changes her mind, you have to find another customer who will pay the same price to cover all the time and money you've invested or else swallow the loss on a large and expensive piece of furniture you may not want or have room for in the first place.

Because an antiques business is frequently described as a dream business, many people enter the field because they think it will provide them with a quick way to make a buck. For that reason, the field does seem overcrowded in some areas, driving up prices in some cases and increasing the competition in others. More people are competing for a steadily-dwindling number of quality antiques in a business where the stakes and the risks can be quite steep.

If you prefer security and risk-free investments above all else, choose another business to start, because your blood pressure and adrenaline levels will be tested in ways with which you will not be comfortable.

Above all, experts advise that the most important way to minimize your risk in the antiques business is to have an eye for what sells within your chosen field.

Spotlight

Hoosier Cabinets

My heart stops whenever I walk into an antiques shop or mall and see a real Hoosier cabinet standing sentry against a wall. These sturdy pieces of furniture served a number of purposes for busy kitchen cooks during the first few decades of this century, and were the first known example of an engineer's efficiency in the kitchen.

Hoosier cabinets are a one-stop kitchen workstation, with drawers, shelves, cupboards, a wooden or porcelain countertop, and a flour bin, all within easy reach. Though more than one company eventually manufactured these cabinets, they were universally referred to as Hoosiers for the first companies that built them. Even though Sears Roebuck and Montgomery Ward also got into the business, all of the smaller manufacturers were located in Indiana, the Hoosier state.

Hoosier cabinets were made of oak and enamel, and, for the time, were models of how industry was doing its part to contribute to the efficiency of the American housewife. Prior to the advent of the Hoosier cabinet, cooks and bakers used to have to run around the kitchen grabbing ingredients and equipment; with the Hoosier cabinet, at least they could stand in one place.

Hoosier cabinets began to lose their popularity in the 1930s and 1940s when the built-in cabinet began to overshadow the Hoosier. But in 1994, Hoosier cabinets are valued at $700 to $1,200 and more. Though some are used for bookshelves or knickknack holders, many are still used for their original purpose.

Action Guidelines

✔ Realize that if you want to run your antiques business as a bona fide business, you'll probably work harder than ever before.

✔ Consider what type of antiques business you'd like to run, as well as the specialty antiques and collectibles you'd like to focus on.

✔ Talk candidly with your friends and family about how your antiques business will change all of your lives.

✔ Expect some risk, as antiques can be a highly volatile, very seasonal business.

Profile

Francis O'Loughlin
Auctioneer
St. Augustine, Florida

Though most aspiring antiques entrepreneurs first think about opening up their own shop before they think of becoming an auctioneer, some might project into the future and consider the field as a distinct possibility. And though you may think you'll be able to deal with nothing but antiques, the reality is a little broader. Here's how one person did it:

What do you do after you spend 30 years as a cop, all the while working on your cattle ranch in your spare time? You become an auctioneer, of course. Francis O'Loughlin spent many years living on cattle ranches and all of his working career in law enforcement. When he gave that up, he got into real estate. He began to see how auctioneering could help his business. In 1990, he went to an auction school that offers a two-week immersion course in the fundamentals of becoming an auctioneer.

"The first thing they teach you is how to speak clearly and let people know you're trying to sell them something," he relates. "I didn't know how tongue-tied I was. It took me two months before I could loosen up enough to lead an auction."

Everything at the school was hands-on, with students attending auction barns and sales every day of the course. "There was constant movement from one instructor to another. Each one has a technique designed to teach you how to handle a crowd," he recalls.

After several years in the business, he's convinced that a good ring man is the most important part of running a successful auction business. "He's the guy gathering the bid," O'Loughlin explains. "The auctioneer is calling the bid, but the ring man is doing the work."

After he left school, O'Loughlin contacted some auctioneers in his area to arrange an internship; he wanted to call
bids or play ring man. "Interning at other auctions—especially benefit auctions—is the best free advertising you can
get," he says.

Many states have very strict rules on licensing auctioneers;
Florida is one of the strictest. After the aspiring auctioneer
passes a test, the state does a background check and conducts
a hearing to make sure the person is not of questionable character. After all, an auctioneer handles a lot of money and is
entrusted with people's goods.

Besides interning, auctioneers can gain experience by going
to other auctions and letting the auctioneers know they're
licensed. They'll give you something to do. "It gives a little
pizzazz to an auction. It also provides the auctioneers with a
break, especially if they're alone," explains O'Loughlin. "Even
established auction houses will put you to work."

O'Loughlin opened his auction business in collaboration
with his partner, Terry Pacetti, who runs a real estate agency.
They average two to eight auctions each month. They conduct several different kinds of auctions. Cattle auctions
require the auctioneer to deliver in rapid-fire because he's
moving a lot of animals. Antiques auctions are slow by neces-
sity.

"The first rule of auctioneering is that you should have
some knowledge of what you're auctioning off," he says.
"Auctions bring people out who normally wouldn't have
known about the items for sale. An auction is one of the best
marketing tools I've ever seen."

Chapter
2

REQUIREMENTS

Okay, you know about all the different kinds of antiques businesses that are open to you, you acknowledge the risk, and you know why you aspire to be in the business. But how do your business goals fit in with your personal goals and values and do you think you have what it takes to make a go of it in this business?

It's time to take a breather and do a little self-evaluation. Knowing your true motivations for entering the antiques business and what you hope to gain from it—both personally and financially—will make it easy for you to be clear about the direction your business takes. More detailed business and market planning comes later, in Chapter 4. For now, it's time for you to take stock of yourself.

Assessing Your Personal Goals

Why do you want to open an antiques business?

Before you reserve a booth space at a mall or a show and even before you pick a name for your business, it's important to know exactly how owning and operating an antiques business will fit in with your personal goals, if at all.

It's a good idea to set aside a separate notebook for the various questions raised throughout this book. You can also use the notebook to jot down any ideas about your prospective business that come as you're reading.

For now, try to answer these questions as fully as possible. Write down everything that occurs to you. And if you go off on a tangent, keep going. Frequently, your best ideas will come when you just allow your mind to wander.

Like any so-called glamour business, there's much more to an antiques business than meets the eye, starting with the amount of time and work you'll have to put into it just to get

- What are your three most important reasons for opening an antiques business? Explain each in detail.

- Do you prefer a lot of social interaction face-to-face or would you rather limit your contact with people?

- What kind of antiques business do you want to start? What are some other directions or methods you may want to add to your business in the future? Are these businesses consistent with your answers to question 2?

- Do you want to start your business part time or jump right into it full time?

- How confident are you in your abilities to buy the right item at the right price? How do you think you'll react when you overpay for an item or are unable to unload it?

- What other personal goals do you have for your life besides owning an antiques business? Do you see your business as a lifelong pursuit, just a hobby, or something to do for a few years until something better comes along?

it off the ground. If you don't want to work hard, either in the beginning or at all, then renting space in a couple of antiques malls will still allow antiques to remain a hobby more than a business for you, since someone else is doing the selling and the paperwork. All you have to do is look for antiques that you'll be able to sell for more than what you bought them for. The downside, of course, is that you won't be able to make much money at it. However, this can be a way to cut your teeth in the business while still keeping it mostly fun.

The reasons why people enter the antiques business are varied: some start as a moonlighting project or second job, others turn to it as a retirement business, while others, who suddenly lose their jobs and need to liquidate some of their assets, see how much money they can make and then turn to antiques as a business instead of looking for another job.

But once you start a business, it may begin to take on a life of its own in a way that may begin to diverge from your personal goals. For instance, you may say you want to start a part-time antiques business, but due to demand for your particular object and a heavy show season, you may find you're spending many more hours on the road and working at home than the 20 hours each week you had originally planned. What do you do? You want your business to remain part time so you can have other things in your life, but you also see that you have the potential to make a lot more money. Most people, of course, would decide to take the money. If you'd like the extra money, but you don't want it to cut into your free time, you can either hire a part-time employee to help you out, or, instead, work full-time during the busy time of the year—generally May through October—and then take the other half of the year off. It's also possible that you can scale back to performing just basic maintenance tasks during the off-season.

It all comes down to the fact that you are running a business and that you have the power to decide how you wish to run it. Some might disagree, saying that any business has the potential to run away with itself, but these are frequently the people who allow the business to run them and not the other way around.

If you want to run your antiques business in a particular way, plan for it and then do it. Many people enter the business because they want to work for themselves after many years of working for other people, but they don't want the burden of people working for them. Fortunately, with a little bit of control and attention, the antiques business is a particularly good business to keep small, with one person or a partner along to help out when necessary.

Assessing Your Personal Values

If you respect objects of value and truly enjoy collecting antiques and other items and if you value the word you give as well as the word of other people, then you'll probably be quite happy in the antiques business.

Which is not to say that there are not people in the business without these qualities. You've already probably heard about how some unscrupulous dealers try to pass reproductions off as originals and succeed at hiding or downplaying an item's flaws—that is, until you get it home and realize it for yourself. All antiques dealers—and even hobbyists—who have been in the business for even a short time have stories to tell about the time they were taken for a ride.

But the vast majority of people in the business are honest and ethical. They have to be or else they won't have any repeat business, which is the lifeblood of the industry.

And this includes you. Even though you will be selling objects to your customers, you will still be providing a service to them. The best antique entrepreneurs pride service to their customers above all else. The fact that you have quality antiques and collectibles to sell is a given. What isn't is the degree of service that owners provide their customers, whether that means shipping an item across the country, spending time chatting with them about a particular collectible, or addressing complaints as soon as they arise.

Unfortunately, in the antiques business, as is the case in virtually all business today, service to the customer usually is *not* thought to be the most important part of doing business. "Well, I have the antiques that everybody wants, so I don't have to be nice," one dealer told me. *Wrong.* Anyone who wants to can find what they're looking for eventually. And yes, this dealer gets business, but from that minority of people who think that buying from surly business owners demonstrates taste. Trust me, more than 99 percent of antiques buyers appreciate good service when they see it in action and will readily reward it with their repeat business. First and foremost, if you subscribe to the belief that the customer is always right, no matter what the consequence, your house list of repeat customers will keep increasing throughout the years.

Just keep in mind how you would like to be treated if you were the buyer.

Assessing Your Financial Goals

Even though the possibility of quick bargains is what lures many people into the antiques business in the first place, it's important to understand that this is not a get-rich-quick business. Such a business does not really exist in any field that I'm aware of. Even if you are able to parlay a dollar item at a yard sale into profits that add up to many times the amount of your original investment, you'll probably do what most people in the business do when they make some money: pay some bills and sink your profits back into buying more merchandise. So while you won't get rich quick, the small and large successes that you'll realize in the antiques business will allow you to expand your operations as well as pay some bills and overhead.

Do your own personal financial goals mesh with the requirements of an antiques business? Answer the following questions in your notebook:

- What would you rather have after 10 years of hard work: A large sum of money in the bank or equity in a valuable home and business that would be relatively easy to sell?
- What's the least amount of money you could live on each month, provided that the mortgage, taxes, and utilities are paid for?
- Do you like doing just one thing to make a living or do you prefer to juggle a variety of tasks?

As I've said before, the first priority of people who go into the antiques business usually isn't monetary; rather, it's a way to convert a much-loved hobby into a profitable business. For this reason, it's possible you may already have the inventory and won't have to invest much money into your business.

When you start out, however, whether it's full or part time, you will probably need to live off some savings or your spouse's or your own income while you're getting your business off the ground. Usually this is because you will need to use any money you make from your business to pay yourself back for the startup costs and also to replace and build up your inventory.

If you want to make a good living while doing something that you love, your own antiques business should produce for you if you start out with reasonable expectations and set up your own personal financial goals at a reasonable level. In order to accomplish this, you may have to branch out to offer a variety of services to your customers. But most antiques entrepreneurs won't mind, as it's one more way that they can continue making a living at what they love.

Assessing Your Risk Tolerance

If you've already been collecting antiques for some time as a hobby, you probably realize that risk is common to the industry and that, once you start seeing it as a profitable venture, you will be exposed to even more risk.

The way to lower your risk in the business is to specialize, but many people just starting out don't have the knowledge or inventory built up yet in order to do this. Even if you do have a high tolerance for risk, it still makes sense to start out small. After all, why open an antiques shop if you're not sure what will sell; and the merchandise you do have will only fill a few shelves; and you don't want to take a lot of items on consignment?

There are many people who dream of opening their own antiques business but will never do it because they don't believe in their ability to succeed. Or else they feel that they won't progress beyond doing a few flea markets a year because they're afraid of taking the big step of leaving behind the security of a regular job and benefits and everything else this affords, even if they are not happy with their present lives. A person who falls into this category has a low tolerance for risk of any kind.

Others are quite used to risk and can't imagine what it would be like to receive a paycheck every week—and this includes me—or are willing to exchange a good part of their security for the freedom of being their own boss. They are attracted to the excitement of running an antiques business and accept the unpredictable income that goes with it. However, even a person who can tolerate risk, even welcomes it to some degree, must recognize that even though everything necessary to operate and promote the business successfully is done, there is still some element of uncontrollable risk to the business, like economic downturns and fickle weather. By accepting this as a normal part of doing business and you can proceed accordingly.

What's your tolerance for risk? Find out by answering the following questions:

- Have you ever run a business of your own before? If so, how did you react when things slowed down? If you don't have experience in running a business, how do you think you would react—with panic or the ability to constantly keep the big picture in mind?

- How would you react and what would you do if you had a slow month in the business and didn't have enough money to pay the mortgage?

- How important is it to you to have material items to validate your self-worth? What would you do if you were to suddenly lose them?

It's important for you to determine how much risk you're willing to accept in running an antiques business. This will influence to some degree the shape that your business will assume, from the specialties you will pursue to the types of business you will conduct and even the limits you will place on yourself when bidding for a particular item at auction.

Frequently, people who go into business for themselves soon realize that the payoff is in the long run, and that in order to do the things that are necessary for their business to succeed, they will have to do without some of the things that they've come to accept as part of their personal lives, like a new car every three years, dinners in restaurants every week, even new clothes. Again, it comes down to priorities, and if you realize that you will be investing a lot of your money back into the business so that one day the business will be a thriving success, you'll see that you can do without certain things in the short term. Many people even decide to finance their antiques business by selling some of their most prized possessions or mortgaging their homes. It's entirely up to you to decide the role that your antiques business will play in your life.

Tools and Equipment

The tools and equipment that are necessary to successfully operate your antiques business depend on the type of business you decide to run. For instance, if you want to become a hauler, you will need a large, dependable truck that will get you where you want to go on time. If you want to run an antiques shop, you will need all the things usually needed to run any retail operation: cash register, display cases, boxes and bags, packing material, and fixtures. If you want to concentrate on doing antiques shows, you usually set up your merchandise in a booth or on table provided by the promoter. However, some savvy show exhibitors spend extra time and money on their exhibits, draping special colorful fabric or artwork on the backdrop, or putting a distinctive piece of fabric on the table to set them apart from the other exhibitors at the show.

But far more important than tools and equipment are the antiques and collectibles you choose to sell, because while you can attract more customers to your business with fancy displays and catchy signs, ultimately, what will make you money are the antiques you choose to sell.

But before you can take the necessary steps to make your business stand out from the others, you have to take note of what others are doing, and then imitate their successes while avoiding what doesn't work for you.

Visit at least five businesses that are similar to the kind that you want to run. Conduct an informal survey, taking special note of what makes the customers flock to one store or avoid another. Play consultant—if it was *your* business, what would you keep, and what would you change? In your notebook, write the answers to the following five questions.

1. What do you like about them?
2. What don't you like?
3. How is each one different from the others?
4. In your opinion, what can improve the physical appearance and tone of each one?
5. Is there anything that seems out of place at any of them?

When you get home, make notes on each one. Which characteristics did you see that you would like to incorporate into your own business? What could you do to make your antiques business different from the others? It's a good idea to spend a lot of time thinking about this last question, because what makes your antiques business unique will help later when it's time to market your business.

Of course, you don't have to let the owners of these businesses know what you're doing. It's a simple matter to find out more information by asking a few questions under the guise that you have a cousin in a distant, noncompeting area who's considering starting a similar business—and what advice would you have for her?

It's likely the owners will open up about their experiences. Since the majority of antiques dealers are not competitive to begin with, due to the cooperative nature of acquiring merchandise in the business, in most cases they will be happy to share their experiences—good and bad—even if they do suspect your cousin story. You also can ask these same questions of the exhibitors at the next antiques show that you attend; many of them run shops as well and they'll probably give you the information you need.

Your market research and interviews will give you further insight into the exact kind of tools and equipment you'll need to run your business the right way from the start.

Financial Requirements

If you plan to start your antiques business from scratch, it won't be difficult to spend $20,000 just on inventory. But since most aspiring antiques entrepreneurs already have sizable collections, the problem usually lies in deciding which objects you can bear to part with.

It will take awhile to get your business off the ground. There's often a lag time between reserving a space in a show and the actual date of the show and between placing an ad and when it finally appears, though in antiques publications printed on newsprint, the lead time can be just a couple of days. You also have to announce your business to current contacts by mail, phone, or in person, as well as scout out new buyers and supply sources.

All this will take money during a period when you are not realizing significant income from the business. So it's a good idea to draw on your savings or a second income so you can set up the business and have enough money left over for food.

At the most basic, your money will go for stationery and other promotional materials like business cards and brochures; for registering your business name with the state; and for a variety of other expenses, depending upon the field you choose.

Much will depend on how large you want your business to be when you start out, your location, the types of antiques you plan to offer for sale, and whether you want to work at it full or part time.

Here's a range of startup costs for seven common fields:

- Antiques shop: $20,000-50,000
- Antiques show exhibitor: $10,000-30,000
- Antiques mall booth: $1,500-5,000
- Mail-order: $500
- Private sales: $1,000
- Picker: $0-100
- Hauler: $10,000

No matter which category you choose, it's important to invest as much money in the beginning as you can and take the necessary steps to set yourself up as a business so you are taken seriously by both your customers and suppliers. If you do nothing else, do this to ensure your potential business success.

Skill Requirements

As mentioned, the most important skill you'll need to successfully operate your antiques business is an eye for what sells and what doesn't. After all, you don't need antiques that will sit in your inventory for a year or more.

Some items will always sell quickly, while others will always take longer to move. If you need to develop your eye for antiques, the best thing to do is to teach yourself. This means working with other established dealers who specialize in your field and will take the time to answer your questions, even if they're elementary. Some fledgling antique entrepreneurs apprentice themselves to a dealer for a few weeks to a year; some work in other antiques businesses and, once well-prepared, only then, strike out on their own.

No matter what your given area of specialty or chosen type of business, there's a place for specific information in the form of associations, books, magazines and newspapers, and especially the suppliers, who will likely buy and sell items to you with great regularity. In fact, suppliers are likely to be the most helpful to you if you present yourself both as a potential customer and as a dealer. Suppliers are usually willing to point you towards even more resources in your specialty and type of business, and may also be able to warn you who to stay away from.

Other skills that you'll need fall under the category of running a business, which any new entrepreneur can learn about from the variety of books on how to start a business. You'll need to learn about cash flow, bookkeeping, and marketing—all of which I cover in later chapters. But again, you can usually learn as you go by experience and by asking other antiques owners what business methods have worked best for them.

Even if you've never run a business before, you probably already know what you're good at from working for other people. And where your skills aren't as good, you'll be able to learn enough to get by. If you can afford to hire someone else to do the work, however, go ahead.

The most important point to realize, however, is that honing your skills for picking antiques and collectibles that will sell will not happen overnight. And if you don't feel confident about your ability to pick salable items, you should wait until you are.

Attitude Requirements

In order to run a successful antiques business, you need to have a flexible attitude. and you should expect it to be tested depending upon who you're dealing with.

When dealing with customers, you have to project an attitude that tells them you're trustworthy, ethical, sincere, and honest about the antiques you're selling them. Your attitude will also be reflected in the prices you charge. If they're priced fairly, your customers will be more confident of their trust in you. If your prices appear high for the merchandise and no amount of haggling can bring about a compromise, then you have lost not only a sale but the potential of future sales, since repeat business is largely built on trust.

When dealing with suppliers and others who want to sell you antiques, your attitude should undergo a subtle but important change. You should still try to project sincerity and honesty as well as the feeling that you're going to be fair in your offering price, but it's a good idea to be a little hard-nosed as well. Rarely in the antiques business, at a show or shop, does an item go for its asking price. At many businesses, there is a 15 percent premium automatically tacked on by the seller to allow room for dickering. Dealers not open to negotiation will clearly state this on the price tag.

You should appear firm when negotiating to buy an item. This attitude is particularly important when you suspect that the item offered for sale or consignment is not what the owner is representing it to be. In this case, you'll be able to take some time to think about it and call the seller tomorrow. Don't let yourself be influenced by people who are pressuring you into buying or to buy an item because the seller needs the money badly. Know in advance that you will maintain your high standards, and your subsequent dealings with both buyers and sellers will clearly reflect this.

Your Assets and Liabilities

Can you now take the risk to start a new business, given the present state of your assets and liabilities—personal and financial—or would it be better to wait a little longer?

Of course, if you're a risk taker, there is no questions about your plan of action. Other people, however, find that they need to proceed more cautiously when proceeding into unfamiliar territory.

If your personal assets lie more with the expertise of certain kinds of antiques rather than dealing with people, even if you can afford to open your own shop now, you may decide to wait until you've budgeted enough to pay for a people-oriented employee who will free you up to concentrate on what you do best.

On the other hand, if you're low on cash but high on ambition, you might decide that either displaying your high-demand items at an antiques mall booth or sharing space with another antiques dealers at the next regional antiques show may get your business off the ground faster than waiting to save up some money.

Learn to know the strengths and weaknesses in all areas of your life. As with any business, if you accentuate the positive and downplay the negative, success will be easier to achieve. For instance, if you think you'll have a hard time ignoring your business to take a much-needed break, it might be a good idea for you to set aside a separate room in your house or apartment for the business so that you can close the door when you need some time away. If, however, you find that you tend to forget about the necessary paperwork of running a business if it's not right in front of your face, you might think about keeping these materials on your kitchen table where you can't help but keep tripping over them and will therefore remember.

Using Technology to Succeed

I find it almost unthinkable to run a business in the 1990s without the modern technological triumvirate of computer, fax, and answering machine; but every so often I hear about the proprietor of an antiques shop who keeps immaculate records on index cards and with a pen and ledger. Especially when a shop carries a large percentage of its inventory in consignment, the time spent on keeping track of everything by hand seems to be a real waste.

Yes, there are still these technophobes around, the staunch holdouts, many of whom see their refusal to convert as a way to maintain some control in a largely uncontrollable world. "I deal with old things all day," they reason and figure that this contact with the past should also extend to the way in which they conduct their business.

For the most part, however, even computer illiterates who show a willingness to update their businesses with technology say, once they make the switch, they wouldn't have it any other way. And those who have worked with computers elsewhere, well, they consider not using a computer tantamount to business suicide.

To manage your antiques business most effectively, you will need word processing, database, and accounting software. If you plan to write and design your own brochure and other promotional materials, there are several good desktop publishing systems that will lead you by the hand through the entire process.

Though both Macintosh and DOS systems have had their day in the spotlight, the popular Windows system is both user friendly and offers access to many more software programs than are currently available for either Macintosh or DOS. Who knows, at some point in the future, you may be corresponding with prospective customers and selling your antiques on the Internet, a vast telecommunications system that allows people to send messages to each other via computer.

As for a fax machine, I would say that it's almost necessary equipment for an antiques business. Not only will many customers make inquiries by fax, but they can also fax their order immediately, along with their credit card number. Certainly, a customer can do all of this over the phone or through the mail, but many more people are used to buying merchandise by fax these days and prefer this method to being put on hold or dealing with a live human being. In addition, by receiving this way, at least you have something in writing should the buyer decide to renege on the deal later.

You have several options when setting up a fax machine: you can get a machine with its own dedicated phone line; you can share the fax with your regular telephone line; or you can send and receive faxes through a modem with your computer. Many people prefer the first option, since both of the others require that you interrupt the use of your phone and computer to accept transmissions. However, it's your choice; computer faxes have the benefit of being able to transmit documents directly from your computer files—you don't even have to print them out first.

Another technological tool you might want to consider is a copier. The personal cartridge copiers will suffice for many antiques businesses that don't make a lot of copies. You could rely on a copy shop, but some owners prefer the convenience of a copy machine within arm's length.

Once your computer equipment is in place, you'll need software to make it work. There are a number of computer programs that have sprung up to meet the needs of antiques professionals in such areas as inventory tracking and customer and supplier lists. There's even an on-line information system called Collectors Net, where you can post items for sale and have conversations with other collectors on your computer.

Here are some companies with software for the antiques business:

Collectibles and Antiques Trading System (CATS)

BDSystems
P.O. Box 1337
Litchfield, CT 06759
203-567-1701

DocuMentor
Elizabeth Poel
809 Devon Place
Alexandria, VA 22314
703-548-9121

Dimark Group
Collectpro
P.O. Box 2797
Murfreesboro, TN 37133
615-896-7692

ByteSize Software
D.A. Heitzman
P.O. Box 4515
West Hills, CA 91308-4515
818-340-5125

BDL Homeware
Bette Laswell
2509 N Campbell, #328N
Tucson, AZ 85719
602-577-1435

CollectorsNet
H Weber Wilson
20 Franklin Street
P.O. Box 1
Newport, RI 02840
401-846-2250

Spotlight

Lenci Dolls

Dolls are big business. There are countless clubs, publications, books, and shows all dedicated to buying and selling antique, and even new, collectible dolls. Surprisingly, many men are avid collectors. In fact, many couples share doll collecting as their passion.

There are Bye-los, Kewpies, and the Kammer & Reinhardt "Baby" dolls that are so ugly they're actually cute. The most unusual dolls ever made, in my opinion, are the dolls from the Madame Lenci Doll Company, which were manufactured from 1919 to 1939 in Turin, Italy. Lenci dolls are especially distinctive for their lifelike animated faces, their size—some models were four feet tall—but especially their eyes: every single Lenci doll glances sideways.

Another distinguishing characteristic of Lenci dolls is their incredibly rich and detailed clothing. Madame Lenci made sure that the dolls she modeled after children from other countries—Spain, Greece, Russia, and Japan, among others—were accurate right down to their shoes. Lenci dolls were also made to resemble such popular celebrities as Amelia Earhart, Jackie Coogan as he appeared in the Charlie Chaplin film "The Kid," Rudolph Valentino, and even Josephine Baker.

Lenci dolls are hard to find, but they're definitely worth the search because of their distinctiveness and artistic merit. Though the Lenci company is still in business, it is these early, original dolls that can be worth up to several thousand dollars and more.

Action Guidelines

✔ Take some time to decide if you're right for the business—and if the business is right for you.

✔ Evaluate whether the slow and steady financial growth of an antiques business matches up with your own financial goals.

✔ If you don't have the stomach for risk-taking, enter the business very slowly and then increase it gradually.

✔ Make a list of the tools and equipment you'll need to open your antiques business.

✔ Figure out how much money you'll need to start.

✔ Decide which tasks you'll assume, based on your own skills, strengths, and weaknesses.

✔ Invest in technology that will help you streamline the operation of your antiques business.

Profile

Pat Owens
Patricia Owens
South Strafford, Vermont

When a chance to "leave the establishment," as she puts it, came around, Patricia Owens packed up and left—lock, stock and barrel—for the sticks of Vermont. Although she had previously worked developing educational programs for the Red Cross in Connecticut, she and her husband jumped at the chance to shed their fancy clothes and lifestyle to live in a cabin with no heat or electricity on 40 acres in Vermont.

"It was wonderful," she said of that first year. "I thought, I'm going to do this for the rest of my life." But soon, she got restless doing nothing and she started to look for a job.

Instead, she found a flea market in nearby West Lebanon, New Hampshire, that rented space to antiques and collectibles vendors for $14 a week. "I came home, went to my closet and saw this fabulous wardrobe from years of working in the corporate world. I'll sell my clothes," she decided. The clothes were snapped up and people asked for more. Since she had exhausted her original supply, she started going to thrift shops and yard sales; she could buy any size she wanted for the first time in her life. Soon she expanded to five booth spaces and was buying from wholesalers.

"I didn't like not being able to be in the space after 5 P.M., so we started looking for a space of my own," she recalls. They found an old general store in South Strafford, Vermont, about 30 minutes from Hanover, New Hampshire and Dartmouth College. "It's in the middle of nowhere," Owens admits. They began to renovate and decorate the space. Upstairs there were two apartments to rent out, which helped keep the overhead low.

"A lot of people say my choice to be in this town was pure folly because of the vision I had in my head: I wanted to play house," she remarks. "I wanted to have an enchanted Alice-in-Wonderland place and I needed space I could afford."

Indeed, Owens' store looks like a fashionable Victorian grandmother's attic, with clothes that are classic and in style. A selection of vintage clothing for men and women is in the basement. The two dressing rooms once served as meat lockers.

"In the beginning I picked what I liked, but I learned as I went along," she says. She spends at least one full day on the road looking for clothes for the shop, hitting junior league shops in Connecticut and other consignment shops in Massachusetts and southern New Hampshire for vintage and other used clothing.

"Sometimes I buy things that will look wonderful in the store, and not because I think they'll sell," she says. And sometimes they don't. She keeps clothes in the South Strafford shop for six weeks; if they don't sell, she brings them to the West Lebanon flea market, where she still has a huge first-floor shop. If they don't sell after a few months, she gets rid of them. "Sometimes clothes get tired and stale, and there's no more room for them. In that case, you have to be ruthless and get rid of them," she indicates. She bags them and donates to the many thrift shops she buys from and prays she doesn't buy them again.

After she had been in business for awhile, she began to take clothes on consignment. The consignor gets 50 percent of the retail price; both locals and visitors bring in clothes. She pays for consignments once a month if they have sold for more than $30, and lets the figure accrue if she sells less than that amount. She also offers a running credit. "Consignors are my partners," she says. She had to learn how to say no nicely when a consignor brings in clothes that are not appropriate for the store. She puts consignor money into a separate account; she knows of some shops that have gone out of business because the owners have spent the money owed to consignors.

She personally handles every piece of clothing she accepts, doing whatever's necessary to make the item presentable, which includes cleaning, mending, and ironing. "I've had people come in and buy back their clothes because they got washed, ironed, and depilled. They said it didn't look like the same piece of clothing," reports Owens. "Part of my business is just that: making something awful look good."

Even though the store is distant, the ride is pretty. "People do exactly what I thought they would do," she says. "Women or couples come here for a jaunt. Some come regularly from 90 minutes away." She limits the hours of the store to give herself time to travel, looking for clothes. "I don't want to be in a store all the time," she adds.

"You don't have to have something for everybody," she advises. "Go with your own sense of how you like it. Do what's fun for you. I've found that the more I do what seems right to me, the better I do."

RESOURCES

E ven though there may be nights after you start your antiques business when you wake up in a cold sweat and wonder what you're doing, when you feel like it's you out there against the elements, you should realize that you are not alone. There are hordes of publications, experts, associations, and seminars and courses that will help you during every step of building your business. And through many of these resources you will also find other people in the business—in your immediate area and across the country—who offer networking and camaraderie. Some of the organizations of antiques dealers also will provide discounts on essential business supplies and services, so you can make sure that more of the money from every sale will be yours to keep.

Your Own Experiences

No matter what kind of endeavor you choose to pursue in the antiques business—or how many—you'll find that the first resources to draw on are your own experiences.

Once you made the decision to start your own antiques business, you may have turned into an automatic note-taking machine, recording what other people who dealt in your specialty were doing and what you particularly liked about it. And if you didn't, the questions you asked yourself in Chapter 2 will help put you in that mode.

Presumably, you're interested in starting an antiques business because you like antiques and have amassed a sizable collection of your own. You may already have sold some of your own collectibles to trade up, but it's probably been on an informal basis. So you already have a taste of what it's like to run your own antiques business and you want more.

It's true that the best way to develop the experience necessary to run your own business is to go out and get started. Now. If you're not already doing it, take every possible moment of free time you have and start haunting antiques shops and malls and attend as many auctions as you can. And if you already frequent these businesses, start looking at them with a fresh eye. Don't just look for items that you'd like to buy, but take a good look at what other people buy and why. At shows, carefully examine the condition of pieces you've never looked twice at before and ask the dealer for a thumbnail sketch of the collectibles. This will provide you with a broad education and the forces that drive the wheels of the antiques market.

When it comes to the antiques and collectibles that will be your specialties, however, it's important to immerse yourself even more than previously in the subtleties and nuances of each item. Join one or more of the organizations that are devoted to your specialty and become an active participant. Learn even more about your specialty than you think you could possibly need to know. Remember, one of the unstated services your customers will be buying from you is your knowledge and experience. As an antiques dealer, you will have performed the preliminary screening for your clients by placing for sale only those items that you deem to be worth it. And the more experience you have, the more finely tuned the screening process will be.

So it's very important to take the time to further your education in a specialty, even when you think you already know everything there is to know about it. Keep learning until you have enough knowledge that you feel you could sit down and, blindfolded, write a book about your specialty. Even then, there will always be more to learn.

Researching Customer Needs

Again, you can use the base of your own experience to determine what your customers will want from you. You may have already figured out that no matter what you collect, there will be others who collect it too and will contact you once you make it known that you offer these items.

So on the one hand, since you already have a built-in audience for your merchandise—and the more popular an item is, the larger your scope—there's not much that you have to do to research what your customers want, since they will come to you. However, good service is what sets any business apart. In order to truly serve your customers—and bring in new customers—you will have to determine the extras that will attract them to do business with you rather than the other business in the county that specializes in Depression glass.

What is important to customers in doing business with a company? Courtesy, of course. But free shipping, the acceptance of every charge and credit card under the sun, extended hours, personal searches, and the impression that you will bend over backwards for them are the major reasons why customers prefer one business over another. Americans are busy these days and anything that you can do to make it easy to shop with you will help earn you their business. In the long run, this also will make it easier on you, since once you win over a customer, they will tend to do all future transactions with you and not one of your competitors.

Strive to make your business the type of operation that you'd like to buy from, as well as a business that makes you happy in all areas, from decor to store policies, even the music you choose to play. If you're satisfied, your customers will be too.

Trade Associations

If you don't subscribe to Groucho Marx's credo that he wouldn't join any club that would have him as a member, then you'll be interested in associations that provide networking and business services to antiques businesses. However, it is the vast number of associations that are dedicated to collecting everything from Uhl pottery to Pez candy dispensers that holds me in awe. More than the general antiques trade associations, these specific organizations are especially for the collector who is an absolute fanatic about a particular antique or collectible. Most of these associations publish periodic newsletters, hold annual workshops and conventions, and can answer members' questions about a specific type of collectible, say, cigarette lighters.

Many of these smaller organizations also will be able to steer you toward repair services, suppliers, appraisers, and museums that focus on your particular specialty. You should also contact and join your state antiques dealers association, if one exists.

Listed below are the major generalized antiques associations, some state organizations, and 25 of the more interesting specialty organizations that exist. Also asking other dealers in the business about them, since there are so many of them—some advertise, others don't.

National Associations

National Antique & Art Dealers Association of America
15 E. 57th St.
New York, NY 10022
212-826-9707

American Antique Arts Association
P.O. Box 426
Temple Hills, MD 20748-2413
301-449-5372

State and Regional Associations

The New Hampshire Antiques Dealers Association
585 Concord Rd.
Northfield, NH 03276

Antique Dealers Association of Maryland
P.O. Box 303
Olney, MD 20832

Vermont Antiques Dealers Association
c/o Murial McKirryher
55 Allen St.
Rutland, VT 05701

Berkshire County Antiques Dealers Association
P.O. Box 594
Great Barrington, MA 01230

Specialty Associations

American Society of Bookplate Collectors and Designers
605 N. Stoneman Ave., No. F
Alhambra, CA 91801
213-283-1936

American Carousel Society
3845 Telegraph Rd.
Elkton, MD 21921-2442
410-392-4289

Compact Collectors Club
P.O. Box Letter S
Lynbrook, NY 11563
516-593-8746

Antique Doorknob Collectors of America
P.O. Box 126
Eola, IL 60519-0126
708-357-2381

International Petroliana Collectors Association (Gas station collectibles)
P.O. Box 1000
Westerville, OH 43081-7000
614-848-5038

National Insulator Association
5 Brownstone Rd.
East Granby, CT 06026-9705
203-658-0353

American Lock Collectors Association
36076 Grennada
Livonia, MI 48154
313-522-0920

The Occupied Japan Club
29 Freeborn St.
Newport, RI 02840
401-846-9024

Early Typewriter Collectors Association
2591 Military Ave.
Los Angeles, CA 90064-1933
310-477-5229

Pipe Collectors Club of America
P.O. Box 5179
Woodbridge, VA 22194-5179
703-878-7655

Antique Radio Club of America
300 Washington Trails
Washington PA, 15301-8210

The Oughtred Society (slide rules)
8338 Colombard Ct.
San Jose, CA 95135

National Stereoscopic Association (View-Masters)
P.O. Box 14801
Columbus, OH 43214
614-263-4296

Antique Telephone Collectors Association
P.O. Box 94
Abilene, KS 67410
913-263-1757

Society of Tobacco Jar Collectors
3021 Courtland Blvd.
Shaker Heights, OH 44122
216-921-0400

Japanese Sword Society of the United States
P.O. Box 712
Breckenridge, TX 76024

The Wooton Desk Owners Society
Richard and Eileen Dubrow
P.O. Box 128
Bayside, NY 11361
718-767-9758

The Frog Pond (frog collectibles)
Ms. Merelaine Haskett
P.O. Box 193
Beech Grove, IN 46107

Fire Collectors Club (Fire Service memorabilia)
David Cerull
P.O. Box 992
Milwaukee, WI 53201

American Pencil Collectors Society
Robert J. Romey
2222 S. Millwood
Wichita, KS 67213
316-263-8419

Griswold and Cast Iron Cookware Association
David G. Smith
P.O. Box B
Perrysburg, NY 14129
716-532-5154

International Swizzle Stick Collectors Association
Ray B. Hoare
P.O. Box 1117
Bellingham, WA 98227-1117

Aeronautica and Air Label Collectors Club (luggage tags)
c/o Aerophilatelic Federation
P.O. Box 1239
Elgin, IL 60121-1239
708-888-1907

Colorado Antique Slot Collectors (slot machines)
John Jerseffy
1420 S. Ivy Way
Denver, CO 80224

Chess Collectors International
Dr. Thomas Thomsen
P.O. Box 166
Commack, NY 11725
516-543-1330

Courses and Seminars

Most of the courses and seminars in the antiques and collectibles field revolve around the identification of reproductions and fakes versus the real thing, how to recognize the differences between an item in mint condition and one with slight flaws, and how to guage the quality of local suppliers and shops.

Many of the specialty organizations listed in the previous section also hold regular seminars and workshops, usually in conjunction with their annual or biannual conventions. In addition, women's clubs and other local and regional social groups frequently will invite a local antiques dealer to speak about what it's like to chase after antiques all the time. However, these luncheon talks have the tendency to turn into one long question-and-answer session with the audience members asking what one of their great-aunt's Victorian hair combs is worth. No one learns much of anything.

Occasionally, I've also seen community and adult schools hold courses on the antiques business, but these tend to appear in major metropolitan areas where the course—usually a one-day affair—is buried deep in a catalog with 499 other choices. Anyway, most courses I've seen involve either identification or refinishing and upholstering antique furniture, not actual buying and selling or what the field is like as a business.

In truth, there are not many courses for the first-hand information you need about what it's like to run an antiques business. One group that offers such a course with any regularity is Vermont Off Beat, a company that runs a variety of intensive weekend workshops. Carol Maurer, the director, hires a local antiques expert to take students to shops, shows, and auctions all weekend, all the while telling stories about the realities of the antiques business and the best way for each student to get into it. Indeed, many of the students are planning to enter the antiques business, either as a sideline or upon retiring from their present jobs.

To find out about the dates of the upcoming antiques workshops, send your name and address to the following for a free catalog:

Vermont Off Beat
P.O. Box 4366
South Burlington, VT 05406
802-863-2535

Perhaps the best known expert on antiques collecting today is Harry Rinker, who became an instant celebrity in the field in May 1994, when he appeared as the sole guest on "Oprah" and discussed collecting with Oprah Winfrey, who is known as an inveterate collector.

Harry Rinker also heads the Institute for the Study of Antiques & Collectibles, which offers a certificate program along with regular seminars and conferences.

Write to the Institute for information on its programs and service:

Harry Rinker
The Institute for the Study of Antiques and Collectibles
5093 Vera Cruz Rd.
Emmaus, PA 18049
215-965-1122

Here's one more company that teaches about the antiques business:

Asheford Institute of Antiques
1552 Hertel Ave.
Buffalo, NY 14216

Books

Depending upon your specialty, there's probably a wealth of books available to help you learn everything you need to know and then some. The books generally explain the history of a particular field and provide plenty of photographs and written explanations about the minuscule, but extremely important, differences between two seemingly identical items.

The more general antiques books that will interest you are the price guides from a variety of publishing companies, usually updated every year to reflect the changing realities—or, as some would say, the fantasies—of the antiques and collectibles market.

There are also plenty of antiques shops directories, annual show calendars, and travel guides. Perhaps the most important guide you could have is *Maloney's Antiques & Collectibles Resource Directory*, which is a fat resource book that's updated every one to two years. This directory lists the names and contact information for possibly anyone in the antiques and collectibles business you'd ever need to know about, or at least those who specialize in a given field. There are more than 2,000 categories of collectibles and more than 10,000 resources you can contact if you want to buy or sell a string holder, visit a barbed wire museum, or subscribe to a newsletter devoted to souvenir spoons. It's not difficult to spend hours with the book.

Many booksellers concentrate on current and out of print books about antiques or your specialty. There are also a number of book publishers specializing in antiques and collectibles, so it would be worthwhile to get on their mailing lists.

Antique Publications
P.O. Box 553
Marietta, OH 45750
800-533-3433

Chilton Book Company/Wallace-Homestead
Radnor, PA 19089-0230
800-695-1214

Dealer's Choice Books
P.O. Box 710
Land O' Lakes, FL 34639
800-278-2637

Green Gate Books
P.O. Box 934
Lima, OH 45802
419-222-3816

Guappone Publishers
RD 1, Box 10
McClallandtown, PA 15458

Herzinger & Company, Inc.
2821 NE 65th Ave.
Vancouver, WA 98661

Mad Anthony Books
800-743-5404

Here are some of the generalist books you should have in your library:

Curtis, Anthony. *Lyle Antique Dealers Pocket Guide.* New York: Perigee, 1993.

Curtis, Anthony. *Lyle's Guide to Cashing in on Collecting Americana.* New York: Perigee, 1993.

Freund, Thatcher. *Objects of Desire.* New York: Pantheon Books, 1993.

Hyman, Tony. *Where to Sell It!* New York: Perigee Books, 1993.

Kovel, Ralph M. & Terry H. *Kovels' Know Your Antiques.* New York: Crown, 1981.

Kovel, Ralph M. & Terry H. *Kovels' Antiques & Collectibles Price List.* New York: Crown, 1989.

Lindquist, David P. *The Official Price Guide to Antiques & Collectibles.* New York: Random House, 1993.

Maloney, David J., Jr. *Maloney's Antiques & Collectibles Resource Directory.* Radnor, PA: Wallace-Homestead Book Company, 1994.

Michael, George. *Basic Book of Antiques & Collectibles.* Radnor, PA: Wallace-Homestead Book Company, 1992.

Peake, Jacquelyn. *How to Recognize & Refinish Antiques for Pleasure & Profit.* Old Saybrook, CT: Globe Pequot Press, 1992.

Rinker, Harry L. *Warman's Antiques and Collectibles Price Guide.* Radnor, PA: Wallace-Homestead Book Company, 1994.

Sloan, Susan. *Sloan's Green Guide to Antiquing in New England, 1993-1994.* Old Saybrook, CT: Globe Pequot Press, 1993.

Walkling, Gillian. *Field Guide to Antique Furniture.* Boston: Houghton Mifflin, 1992.

Magazines and Trade Journals

It seems from the sheer proliferation of magazines and newspapers about antiques that you could easily spend an entire week reading through what's published all over the country, and still not get to it all.

Many periodicals are local in nature, listing upcoming auctions and shows, reporting on recent events, and profiling a specific antiques dealer or collector. Many are crammed with ads, which makes even the weekly papers time-consuming to get through.

The various trade and collectible organizations usually publish a newsletter or trade journal, which will only add to the pile of reading materials you'll want to receive once you get into the business.

Here are just a small percentage of the hundreds of publications that are available to the trade.

American Collectors Journal
P.O. Box 407
Kewanee, IL 61443

Antique & Collectibles
P.O. Box Drawer 1565
El Cajon, CA 92022

Antique & Collectible Marketplace
18055 Beach Blvd.
Huntington Beach, CA 92648

Antique Gazette
6949 Charlotte Pike
Nashville, TN 37209-4208

Antique Review
P.O. Box 538
Worthington, OH 43085-9757

Antiques & Collectibles Business
Moose Mountain Press
RR 1, Box 1234
Grafton, NH 03240

Antique Trader Weekly
P.O. Box 1050
Dubuque, IA 52001-1050

Antiques & Auction News
P.O. Box 500
Mount Joy, PA 17552

AntiqueWeek
P.O. Box 90
Knightstown, IN 46148

Carolina Antique News
P.O. Box 241114
Charlotte, NC 28224

Collectors Journal
P.O. Box 601
Vinton, IA 52349-0601

Collectors News
P.O. Box 156
Grundy Center, IA 50638

Flea Marketeer
P.O. Box 686
Southfield, MI 48037

Maine Antique Digest
P.O. Box 1429
Waldoboro, ME 04572-1429

Michigan Antiques Trading Post
132 South Putnam
Williamston, MI 48895

MidAtlantic Antiques Magazine
P.O. Box 908
Henderson, NC 27536

New England Antiques Journal
P.O. Box 120
Ware, MA 01082

New York Antique Almanac
P.O. Box 335
Lawrence, NY 11559

Ohio Collectors' Magazine
P.O. Box 66
Mogadore, OH 44260

Old Stuff
P.O. Box 1084
McMinnville, OR 97128

Renninger's Antique Guide
P.O. Box 495
Lafayette Hill, PA 19444

Southern Antiques
P.O. Box Drawer 1107
Decatur, GA 30031-1107

Treasure Chest
2112 Broadway, #414
New York, NY 10023

West Coast Peddler
P.O. Box 5134
Whittier, CA 90607

Yesteryear
P.O. Box 2
Princeton, WI 54968

Suppliers

Most of the time, your major suppliers in the antiques business are other dealers who sell to you through antiques shows, shops, and wholesale.

For some aspects of the business, however, you'll need to work with the kinds of suppliers that can help your business run smoothly and will help put your other supplies—your antiques and collectibles—in a much better light.

Most of the suppliers listed here sell only new merchandise. If you don't want to pay a premium for new items, you should ask around to see if other people in the business want to unload a showcase or shipping and packing materials. Frequently, dealers will be willing to part with these items for very little money if they recently left the show circuit to concentrate on their own shop.

Arlington Industries (plateholders)
Arlington, VT 05250
802-375-6139

Collector's House (showcases)
704 Ginesi Dr.
Morganville, NJ 07751
908-972-6190

Collectors Supply Company (bags and plastic sleeves, price tags, etc.)
8415 G St.
Omaha, NE 68127
402-597-3727

J-Mounts/Militaire Promotions(display boxes)
6427 W. Irving Park Rd.
Suite 160
Chicago, IL 60634
312-777-0499

Mega-National Industries, Inc. (tents & canopies for outdoor shows)
Box 538
Round Lake, NY 12151
518-899-6190

Robbins Container Corporation (packing materials)
222 Conover St.
Brooklyn, NY 11231
718-875-3204

Showcases by Lin Terry
59 E. Madison Ave.
Dumont, NJ 07628
201-385-4706

Westgate Enterprises (light bulbs)
2210 Wilshire Blvd.
Suite 612
Santa Monica, CA 90403
310-477-5891

Appraisal Services

From the outset, there are a few things you should know about appraisers: Most states allow anybody who wants to hang out a shingle that says Appraiser to go right ahead and do so.

Since anyone can call themselves an appraiser in the antiques business the term has taken on a slightly shady feel, as many unqualified and unscrupulous people have entered the fray. Technically, an appraiser is an individual who offers a reasonable estimate of the value of a particular item.

That's all that an appraiser should offer you, should you decide to hire one. Unfortunately, there have been a few dealers and antiques business owners who have stretched this pretty straightforward definition to the limits and beyond in order to increase their income, and may offer to buy the item at a discount, offer to sell it on consignment, or charge a percentage of the object's appraised value as the appraiser's fee. Often, these appraisers will lack direct knowledge of your piece and will instead solely rely on readily available price guides for an easy way to collect a fee.

Appraisals differ from a situation where a person walks into a shop and asks the owner if he'd like to buy a particular item and for how much. An appraiser will have no vested interest in determining the value of the piece, while dealers will naturally try to give you the lowest price so that when they resell it, the profit will be higher. Though dealers can also serve as appraisers, they should keep their appraisal services separate from their retail business. Also, appraisers take much more time to arrive at their final appraised figure than a dealer would, who may toss out a number after only a cursory glance at the object. Appraisers will first personally examine and handle the item to check on its condition. They will then provide the client with a written report that includes an analysis of the item's condition as well as its description, and an opinion of the item's value, which can vary depending upon whether you want the appraisal for insurance purposes, resale, or to price it on the open market. The appraiser will charge a fee based on an hourly rate, not a percentage of the item's perceived value.

The best way to reach a qualified appraiser is to check for membership in one of the two national appraisers' societies, which require their members to adhere to high ethical standards. The International Society of Appraisers and The American Society of Appraisers both base their membership on a series of rigorous tests as well as mandatory participation in regular courses and examinations in order to maintain membership.

The International Society of Appraisers
500 N. Michigan Ave., Suite 1400
Chicago, IL 60611-3796
800-ISA-0105

The American Society of Appraisers
P.O. Box 17265
Washington, DC 20041
800-ASA-VALU

Researchers

If you need specific information on a particular item or type of antique and nothing else, you need to contact an antiques researcher who specializes in providing you the details of a particular antique or collectible. This can include information about the creator of a specific style, the historical significance of an object—particularly, *why* the item came into being, or the purpose of an object. Many of the antiques magazines and newspapers have regular columns where readers can send a photograph of an antique or collectible and receive an estimate of the item's value along with a thumbnail sketch of its place in history.

The disadvantage of relying on these columns is that the columnists often have sacks full of letters to choose from and your query might not be deemed to be interesting enough by the writer. Also, many collectors and antiques dealers need to get the information immediately. This thirst for knowledge is one reason why most established dealers have hundreds of specialized and up-to-date books where they can look up a particular item in a flash.

But sometimes the information that's needed is too obscure to be listed in any book, like the exact dates of its creation or a detailed biography of the creator. That's when some dealers consult a research firm that specializes in digging up hard-to-locate information.

This information isn't free, of course, but can be well worth it in order to document the age and authenticity of certain items.

There are a few antiques research companies out there. My advice is to stick to one that does nothing but sell this information to dealers and collectors. As with appraisers who tie their fees and appraisals in with their desire to buy the item, the lines can get a little fuzzy and the ethics can turn questionable.

Here's one research firm with a quick turnaround time:

Antique Researchers
P.O. Box 79
Waban, MA 02168
617-969-6238

Show Promoters

Even if you firmly decide from the beginning that you're going to focus on running your own shop with some mail order business on the side, sooner or later it's likely you will get the urge to exhibit at a show for the increased exposure as well as the excitement of meeting new customers and other dealers.

The process of show exhibiting is pretty simple: Choose a show, send in your check to reserve a space, bring your antiques and collectibles to the exhibition space, and set it up. After the show, you break down your merchandise and truck it home again or head for the next show.

The number of shows are growing every year in all parts of the country. Here's a partial list of the hundreds, perhaps thousands, of show promoters in the United States. Some might run only one or two shows a year, while others may organize one almost every weekend. You can also find the names and addresses of many others by checking out the show ads in the many antiques and collectibles trade newspapers and magazines.

Antiques Extravaganza of North Carolina
P.O. Box 11565
Winston-Salem, NC 27116
919-924-8337

Coastal Promotions
P.O. Box 159
Bristol, ME 04539
207-563-1013

Colonel Larry Stowell Promotions
P.O. Box 175
Mendon, NY 14506
716-924-4530

Country Folk Art Shows, Inc.
P.O. Box 111
Ortonville, MI 48462
810-634-4151

Great Eastern Productions
23 S Seventh St.
Quakertown, PA 18951
215-529-7215

Heritage Promotions
Nine Joanna Way
Kinnelon, NJ 07405
201-838-5223

Jack Black Enterprises
P.O. Box 61172
Phoenix, AZ 85082-1172
800-678-9987 or 602-943-1766

Marketplace Productions
P.O. Box 36436
Los Angeles, CA 90036-9998
213-933-2511

Revival Promotions
P.O. Box 388
Grafton, MA 01519

Steve Jenkins Antiques Promotions
P.O. Box 632
Westfield, IN 46074
317-896-5341

Sy Miller Productions
P.O. Box 967
Rancho Santa Fe, CA 92067
619-436-3844

Small Business Administration

The Small Business Administration, which you help fund with your tax dollars, is a veritable gold mine of information. There are three major divisions within the Small Business Administration that can assist you in the start-up phase of your business, as well as provide you with advice and assistance once your business is up and running.

One is the Small Business Development Center, which counsels entrepreneurs in every conceivable type of business and at every level of development. The SBDC will set you up in private sessions with an entrepreneur who has experience running an antiques business. There, you can ask about any phase of running a business, from marketing to locating suitable financing and keeping the business going in tough times.

The SBA also runs the Small Business Institute on a number of college campuses nationwide. Each SBI tends to specialize in a given field, from engineering to business management, but if you're looking for very specific information, contact the nearest SBI that has the program you want. The SBI offers consulting services, largely provided by students in the program but always under the watchful eye of a professor or administrator.

The Service Corps of Retired Executives, or SCORE, can be an exciting place for you to get information about your business. SCORE officers provide one-on-one counseling with retired business people who volunteer their time to help entrepreneurs get the help they need. Each volunteer counselor has extensive experience in a particular field and is eager to share his insights. SCORE also offers a variety of seminars and workshops on all aspects of business ownership; here, you'll get specific advice about the nuts and bolts of running a business, from bookkeeping to taxes.

The Small Business Administration also has programs to help small businesses get loans, but its necessary to apply through a bank. The SBA then kicks in some of the funds and guarantees your loan for your lender. The SBA also offers a large variety of helpful booklets and brochures on all aspects of running a business.

To locate the SBA and its other programs, look in the white pages of the phone book under United States Government. Call the office nearest you for information about the programs and services they provide locally.

To contact the SBA in Washington, write or call:

The Small Business Administration
409 Third St., SW
Washington, DC 20416

To get in touch with the variety of services, call these numbers for immediate help:

SBA Answer Desk 800-827-5722

If you have a computer and modem, you can go on-line with the SBA at 800-697-4636.

Other Small Business Organizations

Once you start your antiques business, you'll be joining millions of other Americans who own and operate small businesses. Specific questions can pop up and you'll undoubtedly want to network with other entrepreneurs who aren't necessarily in the same field.

There are a number of nationwide associations that provide small business owners with information, specific resources, discounts on business products and services, and the chance to work with other members.

Here's a number of nationwide organizations for owners of small businesses:

National Association for the Self-Employed
P.O. Box 612067
Dallas, TX 75261
800-232-6273

National Association of Home Based Businesses
10451 Mill Run Circle
Suite 400
Owings Mills, MD 21117
410-363-3698

National Federation of Independent Business
600 Maryland Ave., SW
Suite 700
Washington, DC 20024
202-554-9000

American Woman's Economic Development Corporation
71 Vanderbilt Ave.
Suite 320
New York, NY 10169
800-222-2933

National Association of Women Business Owners
1377 K Street, NW
Suite 637
Washington, DC 20005
301-608-2590

National Minority Business Council
235 E. 42 St.
New York, NY 10017
212-573-2385

Spotlight

Dinky Toys

When I was the quintessential tomboy, I collected Hot Wheels. I'd arrange the flexible, iridescent orange track into configurations that would be impossible for any real race car driver to follow, and then I'd send my miniature VW Bugs and Ford Mustangs to their gory fate. Fortunately, like cartoon characters, they could take it.

So could a particular brand of toy cars from a few decades earlier—Dinky Toys. Noted for their great attention to detail, Dinky Toys were rugged, authentic models of Chryslers, Ramblers, and Triumphs, among others. Dinky Toys were made in Britain and France from the 1930s through the end of the 1970s. Semis, vans, tractors, even army tanks were some of the company's other products snapped up by eager children all over the world.

If you should spot a Dinky or two at a flea market or antiques shop, and it should look a bit beaten and battered, snap it up anyway. The surprise in collecting Dinky Toys—or any miniature car or truck—is that if you clean them up and repaint them, their value actually decreases significantly, up to 80 percent in some cases. Today, more people are discovering these top-quality toys; inevitably, the top prices of $150 for common models with their original box will just continue to rise.

Action Guidelines

✔ Use your own experiences to set the tone for your antiques business. This is what will make your customers happy.

✔ Join a local or national trade association for networking opportunities and discounts on supplies and other business expenses.

✔ Subscribe to a few of the magazines and newspapers for the trade.

✔ Contact suppliers to see how you can increase your business by using their products.

✔ Get in touch with the Small Business Administration for specialized business advice.

Profile

Lionel Carbonneau
The Country Loft Antique Shop
South Barre, Vermont

Lionel Carbonneau is a patient man. When he and his wife, Marilyn, were married in 1948, they started to collect antiques, which they both loved. As the years went on, he wanted to get into the business, but with two daughters who Lionel wanted to put through college, his dream was postponed.

In 1972, he was 10 years away from retirement, and he already knew what he wanted to do when he left his job: start an antiques shop. He started to build his inventory gradually, buying from individuals and knocking on doors. "Since I was in sales, I was used to that," he says.

In 1982, he finally retired, but he had to wait just a little longer. He and Marilyn decided to open the shop in a barn that was attached to an old house they had bought in central Vermont, one town over from the state capitol. Lionel needed to fix up the barn. He put in stairs so customers could get to the loft. Then he filled the barn with all of the antiques he had collected over the years.

In 1983, The Country Loft opened for business. The Country Loft specializes in primitives. Lionel says they sell a lot of rope beds. Local people make up most of his business, and they're familiar with the open "by chance or by appointment" policy of many businesses in northern New England that are located in unheated buildings. "We're not married to the business," indicates Lionel. "If we want to take a day off, we do." The $25,000 to $30,000 gross the shop brings in helps to pay the Carbonneaus' taxes and insurance.

The most difficult part of the business is finding good merchandise for the shop. "I still go out and look for things," he says. "I also advertise in the paper saying that I'm looking to buy antiques. People call. They think they have an antique, but they don't. For every five items I see, I'll buy maybe one."

Marilyn waits on customers while Lionel is out scouting. "For a good retirement business, the spouse should be interested in the business," he believes. "My wife and I work together, and I think that's what makes a good business. I could see myself doing it on my own, but we do it better together."

Lionel does a little advertising in the local newspapers. He belongs to the statewide organization for antiques dealers, but he says most of his customers are people who've dealt with him before.

Both he and his wife like meeting the people who come to the shop. He's amazed at the attitude of the people at some shops he's visited. "I've been in shops where I've walked in and the owner is grouchy," he reports. "That's not right. You can't expect that every person who comes in is going to buy something."

He suggests that people who are interested in starting an antiques shop take their time. "Crawl before you walk," he advises. "You've got to know antiques; otherwise, you'll go out and get stung. You have to love it. I'm happy with what we're doing now; I don't want to get too big."

PLANNING

Planning is the key to the success of your antiques business, no matter what its form. I believe that starting your antiques business—or any business—without adequate planning is the same thing as setting out on a car trip through unfamiliar territory without a road map. You'll probably spend a good deal of time relying on the advice of other people to give you information on where to go and how to get there, which may not result in the type of business you ultimately want to run.

Take the time now to plan your antiques business down to the smallest detail. It's the single most important thing you can do for your future success.

Planning to Succeed

Before you open your antiques business, you probably, no doubt, expect to succeed; why else would you start your business in the first place? However, only a handful of entrepreneurs *plan* to succeed, and therein lies the difference.

Planning to succeed means you'll have to envision your antiques business—in what areas you'll specialize as well as the forms your business will assume (shop, shows, or mail order).

With your vision in mind, write both a business plan and a marketing plan. Though many businesses do succeed without a business and marketing plan, your business has a better chance of making it if you do take the time to plot out every aspect in advance, from the appearance of your ads and brochures to the color and size of a storefront awning.

If you plan the details of your business before you make your first sale, you'll have a clear idea of what your business should be like. Advance planning will also provide you with a blueprint, so you can check your progress in order to see if you're on target and on schedule in terms of your business progress. It's important to take the time to plan your business before you start it. If you don't, down the road it may be too late.

Unplanned Failure

Even with the best of intentions and the most detailed business and marketing plans, sometimes an antiques business will fail; or the first year's sales figures will come out as much as 50 percent or more below your initial expectations. It could be that you got caught up in the excitement of planning your business and your early projections reflected this enthusiasm; or it could be that your budget didn't have much room for error built into it. Unfortunately, sometimes events can occur that are totally beyond your control, like a prolonged downturn in the economy or unexpected road construction that diverts tourist traffic for an entire summer. With these unpredictable events, the best business plan will not be able to restore lost business.

The usual reasons that an antiques business will fail are lack of capital and insufficient marketing. Even though most business and marketing plans do account for working capital and adequate promotion, most entrepreneurs who are just starting out vastly underestimate the amount of cash they'll need to pay the bills when times get slow. In addition, they often don't factor in the amount of time they'll need to spend on marketing just to get their business established and then keep their names out there. Another common reason antiques businesses fail is that, despite everything you read about the business and all that you think you know about antiques and collectibles, there's a good chance that you'll greatly underestimate the amount of time and energy the business end of your antiques enterprise requires. Couples who run the business together as a joint venture are frequently surprised at the way the business can come between them if they're not careful. Many times, couples will have radically different management styles—for instance, one may rule by the hands-on method, while the other may prefer to operate on pure emotion—that they dismissed as inconsequential when they decided to start an antiques business. I guarantee that if you don't deal with your operational differences before you start your business, they will come back to haunt you as well as the business.

While you take the necessary steps that will help you to avoid unplanned failure—envisioning your antiques business, writing a business plan, and writing a marketing plan—you should try to address any aspect of your business where you see red flags. For some people, it might be the prospect of keeping only $1,000 in an emergency fund account, while for others it may be when someone suggests that you don't have to worry about bringing extra packing and shipping materials to wrap your merchandise at the end of a show because most people usually sell out their inventories. When you hear things like this, it's a good idea to stop and take a deep breath. Allow these warning signals to give you permission to put some perspective into why you're starting an antiques business in the first place, one aspect that is likely to get overlooked in the frenzy of initial planning. One of the best ways to keep your business from failing is planning to plow all the money you earn from your antiques business right back into the business instead of treating it as revenue you have to depend on to pay the mortgage and taxes. This means that you might have to start by renting booths at smaller shows and malls while you or your partner—or both of you—are still working a full-time job, but many successful and experienced antiques business owners will suggest that you start slow and then expand the business gradually. If you follow their advice, the mistakes you make will usually still be small enough to handle, and you won't panic when you need to invest in a big-ticket item that's essential for you to take your business to the next level.

Envisioning Your Antiques Business

Before you get into the nuts and bolts of writing a business and marketing plan for your antiques business, it's a good idea to take the time now to really think about how you see your business. What kind of antiques do you want to sell? Do you want just a shop in the beginning or do you want to start out with as many balls in the air as you can possibly manage? You might want to answer these questions twice: once for how you envision your antiques business at the start, and again for a year or more later, after you have been able to shape your business closer to what you ultimately want it to be. If you plan to open your antiques business with a partner, both of you should separately answer these questions and compare your answers. If any of your answers differ significantly, you should discuss your disagreements immediately to avoid unnecessary expense and trouble later.

- What would you like to name your antiques business?
- Do you want it to be a part-time or full-time business?
- Do you want to concentrate on low-priced objects, high-priced objects, or a combination, depending upon your customers?
- How much money do you want to invest in your business? To what extent will this determine what you are able to do in the beginning?

- Do you plan to hire employees at the start?
- How do you plan to locate and buy inventory?
- What kinds of customers do you think you'll have? Describe your basic customers in terms of where they're from, what they do, why they want to buy your antiques, and the services they'll need from you.
- What kind of image or first impression do you want to create with your customer?
- What kind of sign will you hang out front?
- What will be on your answering machine announcement? Or will you hire an answering service?
- What other touches do you want to add that will make your antiques business the kind of place you'd like to visit?
- What's important to you when you deal with other antiques businesses? Try to incorporate these factors into your own vision.

And of course, you should ask yourself any other questions that are important to defining your business.

Writing Your Business Plan

Why should you have a business plan? You have a good idea of what you want to do—open an antiques business—the different forms it will take, and when you plan to start it. Even if your goals are less than specific right now, you probably already have some idea of what your ideal antiques business would look like.

Writing a business plan will help you to map out a specific blueprint that you can follow on your way to meeting your goals. A business plan allows for no confusion about any part of owning and operating your antiques business; that's why you'll write it all down. Getting all of your ideas down in writing gives you a detailed itinerary, which could be easy to ignore amid the excitement of starting a new business. And since you write the plan yourself, you'll be able to tailor it to your own needs, while having the freedom to tinker with it later when problems eventually crop up.

Once you have designed and written a business plan, your banker, your suppliers, and other potential business contacts will be able to see what you plan to do with your business in language and figures they can understand. You'll also find that the act of writing reveals a lot of hidden thoughts and ideas that might not have come up otherwise. In addition, you'll be able to get all of the little details about your business down in writing, so there's no question about your intentions when a discrepancy arises.

If you write your business plan before you start to work on other aspects of your antiques business, you'll be way ahead of the competition; most businesses simply do not plan out their strategies so carefully, which will give you the clear advantage. Writing a detailed business plan will illuminate the type of antiques business you want to run and will help you see if your budget matches your goals, if you should wait to start your business until you save up more money, or if you should enter the antiques business at all.

Although a business plan is an important step in starting an antiques business that will eventually be successful, it is also designed for your reference as you proceed in business. If you occasionally check your progress against the goals of your plan, you'll be able to see the places where you need to make some changes. In addition, it will help you determine if you're meeting or exceeding your original goals.

A business plan can be a few pages long or a massive 100-page document that leaves nothing to chance.

Though it takes more time to write a more detailed plan, it's best to err on the side of quantity when designing a business plan for your antiques business. After all, the more you know about your business before you open your doors, the better prepared you will be for the surprises that will inevitably crop up later. Figure 4.1 shows an outline of a business plan.

- **Cover Sheet**—List name of business and all principals along with an address and phone number.

- **Statement of Purpose**—Briefly state your objectives.

- **Table of Contents**

- **Section One: The Business**—Describe the business. What will you provide the customers? Who are your target markets? Where will you be located? Who is your competition? What personnel do you expect to hire?

- **Section Two: The Finances**—Include income projections and cash flow projections. If you're buying an existing business, include its financial history under the previous owner.

- **Section Three: Supporting Documents**—Back up the information in the previous sections. Include a resume of your previous employment history, your credit report, and letters of reference along with any other items you believe will help the reader better grasp how you plan to operate your business.

Figure 4.1: Business Plan Outline

Refer to Appendix A for a sample business plan for an antiques business that a young professional couple is thinking of starting.

Writing Your Marketing Plan

Though you will describe your marketing intentions to some extent in your business plan, developing a separate, detailed marketing plan gives you the same planning advantage in promotion: you'll be able to detail and clarify exactly how you will get the word out about your antiques business.

You will read about a wealth of marketing ideas in Chapter 7, but if you don't have a concrete plan to follow, you may allow marketing to assume less importance in the operation of your business. In actuality, it's one of the most important parts of running your business.

As in your business plan, you'll define your purpose and your target market in your marketing plan as well as identifying the various tools in your marketing arsenal. You'll also determine the size of your marketing budget, which should be both reasonable and aggressive; and you'll select the media through which you'll market your antiques business along with your methods for evaluating results. All this will also help you to design your marketing plan for the following year.

If your not familiar with marketing and can't afford to hire a full-time marketing specialist—and what fledgling antiques business can?—you may find it to be intimidating. Marketing is often an afterthought, a task that is performed grudgingly when an advertising deadline looms or after you attend a trade association meeting and decide that your brochure and other promotional materials look painfully out-of-date compared to everyone else's. And if you concentrate on exhibiting your antiques at shows, you probably figure that advertising is the promoter's job, right?

Wrong. If you want your antiques business to succeed, you have to market it yourself and not rely on anybody else. One way to make marketing your business as simple as possible is to map out a specific plan for the entire year. If you consider it to be set in stone, you won't let yourself off the hook so easily. If you write in your plan that in March and September you'll design and send out a new brochure and price list, and you build the cost into your budget, the chances are that you'll follow through.

The primary mistake that small businesses make in their marketing is to rely on advertising alone. Advertising has its place; however, it often turns out to be the most expensive way to reach customers, especially when your display ad is only one of hundreds in the newspaper or magazine.

Advertising is a known entity with a tangible product—in exchange for your money, you get an ad—but it doesn't necessarily produce the results you desire, which is an increase in the number of customers and their sales. Advertising is easy; You tell the sales rep what you want to say, you write out a check, go over the proof, and receive a copy of the newspaper or magazine. In other words, somebody else does all the work. Spending your time and energy on promotion—whether it's sending out a letter to your mailing list or passing out brochures to all of the tourist businesses in your town—is

---

Advertising—Radio, newspaper, TV, magazines, and directories of various trade associations.

Direct Mail—Sending out brochures to prospective and past customers, writing and editing a newsletter, or sending information to dealers that might do business with you.

Publicity—Sending letters, press releases, kits to the media, and making follow-up calls.

Special Events—Planning special events, working with the chamber of commerce and travel businesses.

harder, and doesn't provide you with a guaranteed entity; i.e., an ad in print. What it will do, however, is provide you with increased exposure among customers. They'll notice you simply because you'll stand out. After all, the majority of antiques businesses take the easy way out and spend the bulk of their annual marketing budget on advertising. With what's left over, they hope to have enough money to print another 1,000 copies of their brochure. In planning your marketing consider each of the following programs and how you can combine them to get your message across.

Developing a strong, detailed marketing plan will help you to take a long-range view so that you can spread your efforts among a variety of marketing opportunities. Your plan will also help you to anticipate certain shows and other events that only happen once a year and to budget for them. But the plan is also meant to be tinkered with along the way. For example, if a special advertising deal comes up in your favorite antiques paper in September but you only have $100 budgeted for the month, or if you hear about an idea that has worked wonders for another antiques business nearby and you want to try it, you will look at November and December and perhaps see you don't have much scheduled in the way of marketing programs even though you budgeted for it. So you take the money from those two months and go ahead with the project.

There will be four different aspects to your marketing plan. The type of customer you're targeting enters into each of these aspects, broken down by region, profession, sex, income, and interests.

1. The amount of time you will spend marketing, on both a daily and weekly basis.
2. The type of marketing you plan to do—magazine publicity, newspaper ads, or revamping your brochure and business cards.
3. The amount of money you want to budget for each month and for the year.

4. Who's going to carry out each task—for some business-es, only one person will be responsible for writing copy, working with a graphic artist, and doing interviews with the press. Even for the smallest businesses, some business owners decide to spread out the responsibilities to insure they get done and to provide a fresh eye.

To draw up your annual marketing plan, you'll have to answer a lot of questions. You'll need to be as complete as pos-sible, however, to design the best marketing plan for your business. Use your antiques business notebook to record answers to the questions in Figure 4.2 on p. 88.

Think about your answers to these questions shown in Figure 4.2 for a few days. Is there anything missing? Refer to Appendix B for a sample marketing plan.

Starting an Antiques Business from Scratch

If you decide to start your antiques business from scratch, whether you use a building you already own or rent or buy a space to accommodate your business, you will need to do more work than if you bought an existing antiques business. The advantage of starting from scratch is that it costs less; the disadvantage is that it will probably take more time to set it up before you are able to open your doors.

There's also a lot more detail and legal work to do if you start from scratch, which includes getting a business license, securing the proper insurance, and setting yourself up as a business, all of which is covered in Chapter 5.

The main disadvantage to starting an antiques business from scratch is that you won't generate income until you open the business. From experience, I'll warn you that this always takes longer than you think it will. While you will initially pay more for an antiques business that has already been up and running for awhile, it will start producing revenue for you from your first day of business. Several owners who started

Figure 4.2:

Market Planning Assessment

TIME

How much time do you spend each week on marketing?

Provide a breakdown of how many hours you'll spend each week on publicity, advertising, direct mail, and other areas. Do you feel this is enough time? Do you think you're using your time effectively?

Would you like to spend more or less time? What would you spend it on, or where would you cut back?

When are your busiest seasons? How far in advance should you begin planning for the various media and projects that you want to do?

Look back over the last calendar year. Which months were slow in terms of business? Which were busy?

MEDIA

In which media would you like to focus more of your marketing efforts?

What type of marketing brings you the most customers?

BUDGET

What percentage of total sales does your marketing budget comprise? How could you increase—or decrease—that amount? What other categories could you take money from?

Do you have an annual or a monthly marketing budget now?

Would you like to invest more money in one or more categories? Which ones? Why?

EXECUTION

Name the person or people currently responsible for marketing. Is there anyone else you feel comfortable assigning additional duties?

Are there additional tasks you could assign to a staff member that you don't like to do or don't have enough time for?

CUSTOMERS

In which area of the country do most of your customers live? Are they urban professional types?

What type of customer would you like to see more of? How can you target them? Why would they be attracted to your business?

their businesses from scratch admit that if they had it to do over again, they would buy an existing antiques business from somebody else. Before you do anything, however, it's a good idea to consider the pros and cons of each as well as your own temperament.

Buying an Existing Antiques Business

If you do buy an existing antiques business, you'll find that most of the detail work has already been done, from the business license to the insurance and the customer list. The only thing you have to do is to change everything over into your name so that you are recognized as the owner of the business.

Even if you buy an antiques business, you'll still need to write a business and marketing plan to make the most of your investment. However, you do have the distinct advantage of a track record to help you gauge your own projected revenues and other facets of the business. There is one particular danger if you decide to buy an existing antiques business that you should know about. Since an antiques shop is such a personal shopping experience for some customers, particularly the ones that make use of search services you may offer, you should be prepared to have certain established customers shun you after you've taken over the business.

Even though your inventory and services may remain the same, some established customers may prejudge you and assume that you lack the eye and good taste of your predecessor.

There are also some customers who wish to show their loyalty to the previous owners of the business by refusing any and all contact with you. I believe, however, that most customers aren't so single-minded and will give you a chance—if you've basically kept the business pretty much intact.

If you buy an existing antiques business, you'll be the beneficiary of a (hopefully) good reputation along with an established customer list. In addition, tourists and other transients may already know about the antiques business by reputation. This group represents yet another pool of potential customers to aim your marketing plan towards.

The most common form of antiques business that is offered for sale is an independent shop. Others—exhibitions at shows, mall booths, or a search service—are best to start from scratch so that you can put your personal stamp on it from the beginning; they're easy enough to start that it really isn't necessary to buy one of these businesses from another business owner.

Frequently, if you buy an existing antiques shop, you may find that you'll actually end up spending less money overall than if you were to start from scratch, once you factor in all of the inventory, fixtures, and other amenities that are included in the purchase price. And if you figure that your labor is worth something (even though you shouldn't plan on paying yourself a salary for a while, so as to reinvest your profits back into the business), you may discover that buying someone else's established antiques business outright may, in the end, turn out to be a veritable bargain.

Evaluating an Opportunity

If you're going to start your antiques business from scratch, you'll have less to evaluate than if you plan to buy a going concern. If you're buying a shop and plan to focus your efforts there, the first—by far most important—thing to consider is the location of the shop. If the building is located in an area where a significant number of transients pass through your town and a strong local buying market is in place, you're pretty much set. It also helps if you're located near a college or private school, or major business district where local workers like to spend their lunch hours. If you plan to concentrate on shows or antiques malls, and don't need a shop, then location is not an issue, you can run the business from your kitchen table.

If you're buying an antiques shop, of course, you should also consider the issue of location, but you'll also need to comb the books and ask neighboring businesses about the shop. If surrounding businesses aren't crazy about the shop, whether or not a new owner is in place, they can create large problems for you and your customers. It's also a good idea to call previous customers for their impressions of the shop, if the current owner will release the names.

Even after all this, however, deciding whether or not to start your own antiques shop or buy an existing one will depend on your own feelings about it: If it feels right, then go ahead and do it.

Spotlight
Stock and Bond Certificates

If you regularly invest in the stock market today and sometimes think that the company shares you own are only worth as much as the paper they're written on, you should consider collecting stock and bond certificates for companies that no longer exist.

Even though they no longer have any value as a share of stock in a particular business, the chances are that these certificates are worth something on the open market. *Scripophily* is the art of collecting stock and bond certificates and, depending upon the condition of the paper, the detail and artwork on the certificate itself, and the person who signed the stock, you could be holding a piece of paper that is worth some money.

While certificates from the period 1830-1930 are most in demand by collectors, stocks that were issued during historically significant periods—like the Civil War and the Gold Rush—have even more value. Some certificates have detailed illustrations that serve as snapshots of these times, from engravings of the U.S. President to scenes of mines, trains, factories, and other industries. Most collectors choose a particular theme, like oil stocks, before a certain year or from the western states only. Though stocks with autographs from a Rockefeller or Andrew Carnegie can be worth up to $1,000, most old stock and bond certificates are worth less than $100.

Action Guidelines

✔ Plan to start slowly when you open your antiques business, and build gradually from there.

✔ When planning your business, try to describe your venture down to the smallest detail.

✔ Write your business plan for your antiques business.

✔ Write a marketing plan for your antiques business.

✔ Determine whether buying an existing antiques business or starting from scratch would make the most sense for you.

Profile

Nan and David Pirnack
Boulder, Colorado

Though Nan Pirnack had been in the antiques business for almost 20 years with a small shop of her own, it wasn't until her husband, David, retired from IBM that they were able to turn their shared passion into a thriving business. Neither one had liked working in a shop, so they decided to concentrate on the show circuit.

They took part of Dave's retirement settlement and instead of buying an RV like many retirees, bought a truck to haul the antiques from show to show. It's a Ryder cube van, which is 15 feet long, seven feet wide, and seven feet high.

The Pirnacks buy their antiques from many sources at home and when they're on the road traveling. "We'll buy an item when we think we can sell it for a greater amount of money than the person who has it for sale," he explains. "We've also built up a network of pickers who don't have shops and don't do shows. They like to find pieces and sell them to local dealers or people like us, who are passing through."

In addition, Dave finds items in one part of the country that aren't particularly popular there but are somewhere else. For instance, Western items are reasonably popular all over the country, but they're especially popular in the West. They also tend to be less expensive if you buy them elsewhere. The Pirnacks buy antiques from people they meet at the shows. They buy very little from garage and yard sales because items from household sales tend to be newer than what they sell. If they find an item they know another dealer would like, they buy it and sell it to the other dealer. There's much less competition among dealers than is commonly thought. "If you specialize in an item, you know more about its value and worth. You build up a base of customers who are looking to buy what you carry," he explains.

When the Pirnacks buy an antique, the first thing they do is polish, repair, or refinish it. Then they decide which show would be most appropriate to take it to. Nan and Dave travel to about 18 to 20 shows all over the country each year. Some shows they go to every year; others they try out for the first time.

"We'll decide to do a show by talking with other dealers to see how they've done there. We also ask whether they think our type of merchandise would sell well at the show," says Dave. "Sometimes our own customers tell us we should do a particular show as well." Of five new shows they exhibited at in 1993, they'll go back to only two of them the next year.

The size of the booth used at a show and whether there is another show nearby are also factors in their decisions. "We generally will not go to a show unless we can get a booth that's eight by 20 feet," says Dave. The minimum is 8 by 16; they have displayed their antiques in a space as large as 30 by 8 feet. Some shows have full walls with quality wallpaper, if they don't, the Pirnacks bring their own.

"We try to bunch our shows so we don't have to do so much travel," he says. "We just got back from two shows, one in Birmingham and the other in Atlanta. We only made one trip, doing the shows on successive weekends."

Exhibiting at a show requires much more than just showing up and being nice to the people who stop by your booth. Depending upon how elaborate you want your booth to be, it can take up to three days just to set up. The shows last from two to four days, and then you have to break everything down and travel to the next show.

Booth fees range from $150 to $2,200 for the duration of the show, and the Pirnacks budget $100 a day for expenses on the road. Some shows charge admission, while others don't. All are open to the public and the number of exhibitors can range from 30 to 1,200.

"Our style has changed over the years," remarks Dave. "For a while, we sold a lot of pure American country antiques; then we went to Western items, then sporting items. You have to keep up with the trends, but a lot of it is determined by what you can find."

The Pirnacks have been selling antiques on the show circuit since 1989, but they say they paid their dues for the years that Nan had her shop. "You have to know something about antiques before you go into it as a business," warns Dave. They keep a library of 500 reference guides and a variety of trade publications handy to research different items.

"The biggest challenge is finding the best items," he remarks. "You don't find the really special items very often."

STARTING UP

How you handle all the details of starting up your antiques business will probably be the test of whether your business will make it. After all, it takes a lot of work to get up and running before your first official day of business. If you're still excited about your antiques business after you've done everything to prepare for that day, then you have what it takes to get you through the tough times ahead.

Even if you are slightly less than enthusiastic about your business because you've caught a glimpse of the difference between having a hobby and running a business, you shouldn't worry. The moment you make your first sale or see your first repeat customer will bring all those feelings back to you.

Take the time now to attend to all the details that will get your business up and running and you'll have it much easier later on.

How to Test Your Business Idea

The best way to see if your antiques business is a viable prospect, whether you buy an existing business or start from scratch, is to talk with others who also operate antiques businesses, both in your geographic area and your field of specialty.

As I've already suggested, it's a good idea to visit other antiques shops to see how others do it and who your competition is. You might want to visit them a second time and tell them of your plans. Some will do their best to discourage you. Others will welcome an additional antiques business in town, which will tend to attract more customers who may balk at driving 20 miles off the interstate to visit one antique shop, but not several.

If the owners are receptive, ask about any voids they think need to be filled in the area. They may not handle furniture in their shop, but customers may frequently request it. In this way, both of you will benefit.

It's also a good idea to talk to the local chamber of commerce as well as the regional and state antiques dealers associations. Talk to the members of both—local chamber of commerce members usually display a sticker on their doors, while most state associations publish a directory of members they'll send to you without charge. The state associations and chambers may give a different perspective than the local business groups since they have a broader perspective about commerce in the state; the state association can also compare business in your area to other parts of the state and they can usually provide figures and statistics that will tell you if they foresee growth or stagnancy in your area.

Frequently, these organizations hold meetings and seminars to show members how they can increase business and run their operations more effectively. So, while you're still in the start-up phase, it definitely pays to make your contacts in advance and become a member of these groups before you even get your business off the ground.

Selecting Your Business Name

Some people think that a cute name works best in the antiques business, while others take the straightforward approach and name it after themselves.

As a rule, you should pick a name with which you feel comfortable and which best conveys the image you desire. For example, one business that specializes in antique clocks is called Timepiece Antiques. The name has a good flow to it, it's simple, and there's absolutely no confusion about the function of the business. With antiques shops that are located in the countryside and attract mostly tourist business, you'll find names like The Country Cow, The Antique Barn, and Spinning Wheel Antiques. Antiques businesses with these types of names tend to specialize in rural items that are relatively inexpensive. I'd guess that for most of these the business stays in the shop and may be a seasonal venture.

Businesses with more formal names—Woodbury Homestead Art, Goslar-Rock Antiques, and even unnamed shops where only a sign reading Antiques hangs outside, or any shop that contains the names of one or more owners—tend to also offer items that are more refined and expensive; I'd guess that they probably don't limit themselves to just doing business in the shop.

Of course, there are many exceptions to these general rules, but by and large, the name that you choose for your business will help set the tone and pace of your business.

Pick three or four names then try them out on friends who will be honest with you, as well as the people at the local chamber of commerce. All this assumes that you're starting your business from scratch. If you're buying an existing business, my advice is to stick with its current name. Change it only after a few years when you've established yourself. However, by that time, you probably won't want to.

Registering Your Business

As is the case with any small business, the law requires you to meet certain qualifications before you can operate as a bona fide business. Since you are in essence, a retail business, selling items and providing a service to your customers, the requirements are quite simple.

The first thing you need to do is register your business with the state. You will be charged a fee of between $50 and $250 for this. The purpose of business registration is to make sure that there are no other businesses that are currently operating in the state under your name. If so, you will have to find another name for your antiques business. Registration will also alert the state to expect tax revenue from your business. If you don't file a tax return with the state every year, they'll know where to find you.

Licenses and Permits

Before you spend one penny on renovations or upgrading and increasing your inventory of antiques and collectibles, you must check with the local, county, and state business authorities to find out about the various kinds of licenses and permits required and the fire, health, and building codes you'll need to meet, especially if you plan to operate a shop. If you neglect any one of the necessary steps to operating an antiques business in your town, the government authorities on any level will have the power necessary to shut down your business or force you to do whatever is necessary to bring your business up to code. Of course, the best time to find out all the requirements is *before* you open for your first day of business. And you must do this even if you're buying an existing business as the codes may have changed subject to a grandfather clause since the owners started their business; Grandfathered exemptions may well expire when a new owner takes over the business. Or the town fathers may have looked the other way because the previous owners were friends or family; but you can bet that they're going to make sure you dot every *i*, especially if you're a newcomer to town. If they catch you later, they probably won't let you use your ignorance of local regulations as an excuse. In every case, it pays to do your homework first. Ask other antiques business owners about all the necessary regulations in addition to checking with the town and state. Either may overlook something, so it's also a good idea to check with the state's antiques dealers association; ask another antiques dealer for the contact name and number.

Requirements vary from town to town and from state to state, so I will describe only the general purpose of the licenses and permits you will be required to get. Bear in mind, however, the stringency of these requirements will also vary as well. States and regions with more highly regulated governments tend to be pickier about the quality of your proposed antiques business and the fees they charge you for the privilege of doing business will definitely reflect this. Even though you may resent all the legalese and paperwork, it's important to meet all of the requirements. No one says you can't complain every step of the way, however. Below is a rundown of the basic requirements.

- In addition to business registration, some states will require you to have a license to operate as a retail operation.

- You'll need a sales tax certificate from the state to collect tax.

- If you're going to operate a shop out of your home or in an adjacent outbuilding, you'll probably need to have the local fire inspector check the building for properly marked fire exits, an adequate number of smoke alarms, and to check if your house is adequately constructed and protected against fire. In some cases, an older building will meet the local fire code, but if you plan to renovate the structure or if you build an entirely new building, recent codes tend to be more stringent and may require you to construct special firewalls designed to restrict the spread of fire. Hard-wired smoke and fire detectors are a must in most new construction or renovations, as well. Some fire codes may even require expensive sprinkler systems along with a fire alarm system.

- Check the zoning restrictions for your location. Your town government determines zoning and is also responsible for making exceptions for antiques shops and other businesses that are located outside of commercial zones. Though your antiques business will provide a tax base for your town and help promote tourism and commerce, if it is a commercial enterprise operating in a residential area, you will probably have to apply for a zoning variance. The rules do sometimes get creative, though. Some towns will allow you to operate as an antiques shop or business in a residential area as long as you don't put a sign out, or if your sign meets certain standards. You may also have to expand your driveway and parking area to accommodate an increased number of cars.

And far more interesting laws governing antiques businesses undoubtedly exist in individual towns. That's why it's important to check all of the requirements *before* you do anything.

Choosing a Legal Structure

While talking with other antiques dealers, it's also a good idea to ask about their legal structure, whether it's a sole proprietorship, partnership, or a corporation. Each has its advantages and disadvantages and each owner will have their own very specific reasons for picking one over the others.

Sole Proprietorship

A sole proprietorship is the form of business that most single-owner businesses pick. It's easy to start—all you have to do is register with the state and you're in business; you make all the decisions yourself; and besides zoning and other regulations connected with running an antiques business, you're pretty much free from complex laws regarding the operation of your business. You alone are responsible for the success or failure of your business and any profits your antiques business earns are reported as income in your name.

However, because there are few restrictions on a sole proprietorship, when you run into legal or financial trouble, it also falls on your shoulders. For instance, if a heavy piece of furniture falls on a customer in your shop, you can be sued personally; any savings or investments you have—including your equity in the business itself—is fair game for the customer and a hungry lawyer who sees your established antiques business as a piggy bank that needs to be shaken.

For many antiques businesses, the amount of liability coverage normally included in your business insurance policy will be sufficient to handle a "reasonable" lawsuit and settlement. The remote chances of being hit with a lawsuit and the relative ease of operating this form of business ownership make a sole proprietorship the preferred method of business organization for most antiques business owners.

However, if your business should fail, you will be responsible for all outstanding debts incurred during the course of doing business. Failure to pay debts or declaring bankruptcy will be reflected on your personal credit record.

Partnerships

A partnership is essentially a combination of two sole proprietorships. This means that while the strengths are doubled, so are the inherent weaknesses.

The owner of an antiques business will frequently decide to create a partnership and start their venture with a friend or business colleague. Married couples sometimes decide to form a partnership for their antiques business. Though a partnership means more energy and money for the business than a sole proprietorship, it should be entered into with extreme caution. The best partnerships work when the partners have complementary talents and one leaves the other to do what he or she does best. For instance, one partner may have a background in marketing and day-to-day business operations, while the other excels at finding items to sell for a profit in the shop and at shows. As long as each trusts the other to concentrate on their department and interfere only when problems arise, then the partnership will probably do well.

Partnerships usually run into trouble when the partners have similar skills or different ideas about the right way to run a business. For example, when both partners want to be responsible for searching for items to add to the inventory and neither wants to do the bookkeeping or marketing, you can bet that there are going to be problems right from the start.

As with a sole proprietorship, if a customer decides to sue your business, both partners are personally liable. And if the business fails, leaving outstanding debts, again, you are both responsible. You should also be aware that if one partner disappears after an antiques business goes under, the other person is held responsible for all the debts. Even though this is rare, you should be aware that this could happen; undoubtedly, you will hear about similar horror stories in your travels.

Corporations

A corporation is best defined as an inanimate object, a business organization with its own needs aside from those of the business itself and subject to financial and legal restrictions. It's more difficult, expensive and time-consuming to form and operate your antiques business as a corporation, but it also absolves your formal, personal responsibility in case business sours or a customer or supplier decides to sue.

Another advantage that corporations have over partnerships or sole proprietorships is that they can raise money by selling shares in the business; the only recourse the other two forms have is to borrow money from a bank or from friends.

But a corporation is by nature more unwieldy than the other two because it does have some responsibility to its shareholders, who are really considered by the law to be part-owners. The IRS taxes corporations on a different scale from sole proprietorships and partnerships and there are even more rules and regulations a corporation must follow on both the state and federal levels. Except in the case of a Sub-Chapter S corporation, corporate income is taxed twice—first as income to the corporation, then as dividends to individual shareholders. There are also certain restrictions on the types of operations a corporation can run—some expansion and growth issues, for example, require the approval of stockholders before a project can proceed.

Some antiques business owners automatically opt for incorporation to protect personal assets. In part, the type of antiques business that lends itself most to incorporation is one with more than two owners. Ownership issues and the decision-making process become more complex and unwieldy when there are more than two owners. It's naturally easier to rely on a board of directors and group of stockholders to help make vital decisions concerning the day-to-day operations, especially since they've invested their money and trust in the business. Besides, sometimes the principal owners are so close to the business that they can't see the forest for the trees; this is another way that a corporation can help the business.

Do You Need an Attorney?

Whether or not you choose to use the services of an attorney to help you start your antiques business depends on how you view the legal profession and how detail-oriented you are. Some antiques business owners swear by their lawyers and consult with them about every decision that needs to be made. Others swear *at* them and will never use an attorney for anything in their business or personal lives if they can possibly avoid it.

The happy medium lies somewhere in between. If you're planning to incorporate your antiques business, you'll probably need to use a lawyer. Although more people are learning how to incorporate themselves, the vast majority use a lawyer to help facilitate the process.

If you're buying an existing antiques business or a separate building to use for your antiques business, you will undoubtedly have to hire an attorney to do a title search and to help prepare a warranty deed for the property. But aside from these tasks, you will probably be able to do most of the tasks involved in starting your antiques business without the services of a lawyer.

Do You Need an Accountant?

If you're unsure about the type of business organization that suits you best—sole proprietorship, partnership, or corporation—it's a good idea to consult with an accountant to help you decide. An accountant will analyze your current financial situation, help you determine what you want to gain from your antiques business—equity or income—and advise you about how to best achieve your goals.

An accountant can also analyze the books and financial records of an existing antiques business that you're considering purchasing. It's a good idea to find an accountant who has some experience working with retail businesses; you may want to ask other antiques business owners in the area for the names of their accountants. Then call several accountants and interview them to make your choice.

An accountant can also help you set up a realistic budget and a schedule of projected revenues. And if this is the first time you've run a business of your own, these professional services can familiarize you with different accounting methods and the tax rates based on projected revenue and the tax codes of your state. An accountant can also recommend methods of bookkeeping that will make your job that much easier when tax season rolls around.

Insurance for Your Business

Before the antiques business became one of the so-called glamour businesses in the 1980s, most entrepreneurs in the antiques field relied on their standard homeowners' policy to cover themselves in case any part of their inventory was damaged by theft, fire, or other means. Besides, most antiques business owners ran their operations out of their homes, either setting up as a shop or traveling to shows. Unless you had significant damage and corresponding loss of income, insurance companies generally looked the other way and paid for any damage.

Today, it's a different story. As more home-based and small outside businesses contribute a significant amount of revenue to the nation's GNP, a separate business policy is almost mandatory for any antiques business.

There are several kinds of insurance policies that you should carry for your antiques business. First you should check with your own insurance agency to see if it will provide insurance for your business. You should also check to see if your current homeowners' policy has any restrictions, because some companies prohibit their clients from operating any kind of small business on the insured premises. If this is the case, you should switch policies, agents, or carriers until you find one that will cover your antiques business.

If you can arrange for one insurance company to cover all of these different kinds of policies for you, you'll probably save money. The premium you'll pay will also be affected by the deductibles and coverage you choose, and can vary from a few hundred dollars up to ten thousand or more.

Spotlight

Gasoline Company Memorabilia

When I was growing up in the '60s, one of my most valued possessions was an AM transistor radio that my father received for free by filling-up at the local Sinclair gas station.

It was no bigger than a pack of cigarettes and had a tiny imprint of the Sinclair dinosaur just above the radio dial. I suspect that somewhere along the line, it was sold for a quarter at one of our many garage sales. I hate to think about what it would be worth today, because all kinds of collectibles from early gas stations—and even those of only 20 and 30 years ago—are appreciating in value every day.

Gas company memorabilia includes the gas globes that once perched on top of every gas pump, promotional signs, giveaways like my prized radio, even oil cans and old road maps.

At an auction in the spring of 1994, gas globes—many of which feature pictures of airplanes—brought prices of close to $10,000, though most ranged from $2,500 to $5,000. Some collectors like anything that has something to do with a gas or oil company, while others specialize in advertising items or products from a specific company, like Mobil or Shell.

And if anyone has an old Sinclair radio, write to me in care of Upstart.

Action Guidelines

✔ Research the local market regarding the need for your antiques business.

✔ Pick a name for your antiques business.

✔ Find out about the legal requirements you'll have to meet, from license and permits to zoning exemptions.

✔ Determine what form of business you'd like—sole proprietorship, partnership, or corporation.

✔ Contact your insurance agency—or an agency that specializes in insuring antiques businesses—about any additional coverage you may need.

Bob Ericson
Lilac Hedge Book Shop
Norwich, Vermont

Book lovers are a breed just a bit apart from other folk, but used book lovers are a species unto themselves and you can spot them a mile away. Those with a particularly acute sense of smell can sniff them out; their musty scent of books gives them away every time.

Bob Ericson opened the Lilac Hedge Bookshop in Norwich, Vermont, in 1983 with his late wife, Katherine. Years earlier, when they were living in Putney, Vermont, they opened the first Lilac Hedge, named for the row of lilacs that ringed the shop. When they heard about the impending construction of a new federal prison just down the road, they began to look elsewhere in Vermont.

They wanted to be surrounded by cosmopolitan people even though they were in the country, so they settled in Norwich, across the Connecticut River from Dartmouth College. "College towns are good places for used book shops," he remarks. "We don't get a lot of students coming here, but just about everybody who got out of Dartmouth wants to come back to the area. And a lot of them are readers."

The Ericsons originally got into the used book business because of their kids. "I'm a compulsive reader," says Bob. "When we sat down at breakfast, I read the labels on the cereal boxes. We always had a lot of books. We had so many that our kids said, 'Why not start a bookstore?'"

So they did. Many people start out in the used book business buying books they like. However, according to Bob, there's one lesson you learn quickly if you don't want to starve. You find out that a lot of books you like don't sell at all.

"Normally, we sell a brand-new book for no higher than 50 percent of the published price, and probably only a quarter of that," he indicates. And a book that sells for $20 new, he sells for four or five. "I hope people do keep buying new books because otherwise there wouldn't be any old books for me," he points out. "At used bookstores you find the good ones, since they've already been through a sorting-out process."

Bob also sells some of the paintings hanging in the bookstore and in the adjacent living room. He'll point out some other items for sale, like an oil lamp from the USS Constitution, an antique bed warmer, and some wood carvings.

Bob does searches for customers, as do most sellers of old and new books, but he likens the process to throwing bottles with messages into the ocean. He considers himself lucky if one in four searches is successful. This isn't very hard to understand when he describes the desired books.

"I get asked to do searches on some very old, fairly esoteric, philosophy books," he says. The most unusual search was for an ancient book on horses by a Byzantine writer. Another was for a copy of Alex Wilson's *American Ornithology*, he found a second edition of nine volumes, which he sold for $6,000— the most he's ever sold a book for.

Chapter
6

OPERATIONS

O perations—the day-to-day routine that you'll set up and follow in order to maintain some degree of order in your antiques business—is not the most fun or creative part of your business, like going to auctions or conducting a search for a customer. In fact, most entrepreneurs will readily admit that operations is downright boring.

Nevertheless, you should consider operations to be a critical part of your business. If you open your business and proceed to run your daily operations in a haphazard way, you're taking one of the fastest roads to driving your antiques business into the ground. Take some time now to set daily operations policy; later on, it will mean that you'll have more time for the fun stuff.

Estimating Operating Costs

Every business has cycles when business is booming and times when it seems to stop dead in its tracks.

But the antiques business, dependent as it is on certain shows and, in the case of a shop, times during the year when there are more people passing through your area, is well known for its ups and downs that can radically swing back and forth several times or more a year. The bad news is that some expenses—like the mortgage or rent and utilities—remain constant. That's why many owners of antiques businesses branch out into different fields, spreading their business out more evenly during the year. For this reason, some owners decide to concentrate exclusively on performing antiques searches for their clients, a sideline that tends not to be as seasonal as other types of antiques businesses.

If you are purchasing an existing antiques business, estimating your operating costs will be easy. Just ask the current owners for a full year's breakdown of expenses along with the current income statement. If possible, go through the expenses with the owners, asking about the budgeted amounts and the actual expenses. Also figure in your monthly loan or mortgage payment on the business, if applicable. If you are starting from scratch, it will be a little more difficult to project the costs of doing business. You may want to ask another local antiques business owner with a similar business about monthly expenses. If this isn't feasible, you'll have to guesstimate your expenses and then adjust them as you go.

Figure 6.1 (pp. 116-117) is a chart that contains all possible expenses you may encounter in running your antiques business. Not all of them will apply for some businesses. I won't provide estimates for the expenses, since they can vary widely depending on the type of business, the kinds of antiques you carry, whether you choose to work at home or rent a space, and so on. It's a good idea to chart out your expenses for each month for a year in order to anticipate which months will have bigger expenses than others. Remember that some are optional, and the more things you can do yourself, the more profit you'll eventually be able to show.

Keeping Good Records

In order to know how much money you have coming in and what you're paying out in expenses, it's important to always keep track of your expenses and various sources of revenue. On the one hand, it will streamline your job at tax time, but it's also enlightening to compare spending in a particular category with the previous year and consider possible adjustments.

There are as many ways to keep records as there are owners of antiques businesses. Some rely on one of several computer programs specially designed for antiques businesses, while others stuff receipts in shoe boxes then dump them out and add it all up at the end of the year.

No matter what record-keeping method you choose, you should make it easy and organize the process so that you can reconcile your income and expenses immediately instead of saving up the work to be done in one lump at the end of the week—or month or year. If you're like most antiques business owners, there's a good chance your spare time will be at a premium once you get your business up and running.

Keeping good records will also help make it easier to figure out the deductions you're entitled to take at the end of the year. And in the unlikely case of a tax audit somewhere down the road, you will help your case immensely if you can show the auditor receipts that will answer all questions about the revenue and expenses of your business.

Good records will track your monthly and annual sales figures to date as well as how each new customer hears about you. This information is important when you're planning future marketing campaigns, because you'll know which ad or promotion brought in enough business to pay for itself.

Keeping adequate records just makes good common sense, too. At the very least, you should get a ledger book to categorize every penny you spend on expenses. Some business check-

The Building

Mortgage _____

Taxes _____

Insurance _____

Utilities _____

Heat _____

Repairs (anticipated)

Office Expenses

Telephone _____

Separate fax line _____

Credit card commissions _____

Postage _____

Stationery supplies _____

Printing _____

Advertising _____

Travel agency commissions _____

Trade association dues and memberships _____

Show Fees _____

Accountant and attorney fees _____

Contract employees, freelancers,
   or consultant expenses _____

Shipping and packing materials _____

Figure 6.1: Cost Estimate Worksheet

Company Vehicle

Loan   _____

Registration   _____

Insurance   _____

Gas   _____

Employee Expenses

Payroll   _____

Taxes   _____

Insurance   _____

Workers' compensation   _____

Bonuses   _____

Discounts   _____

Inventory

Antiques and collectibles   _____

Fixtures   _____

Showcases and exhibits   _____

Figure 6.1 continued: Cost Estimate Worksheet

ing accounts even offer a built-in ledger that allows you to break down the checks you write into different expense categories, eliminating the need for a separate ledger.

Pricing Your Antiques

Pricing is one area of your business that will be wide open. Antiques and collectibles are priced largely on collectors' perceptions as well as what the market will bear. The rules applying to other retail businesses are basically thrown out the window in any antiques business. You will have some items that you will mark up 100 percent, following the lead of other retail businesses in your area; however, since the acquisition costs of antiques vary so widely and can change so quickly, many times you'll find that you have to rely on your gut instincts as well as your familiarity with a particular field.

For instance, you might see a vase in a lot that's offered at auction and figure that whatever you pay for the lot, as long as it doesn't go over $150, will be worth it, because just last week you read in *Maine Antique Digest* that another dealer just sold a similar vase for $100. Besides, who knows what else is in that box? Plus, you have a regular customer who collects anything made of purple slag, and you're pretty sure that she'll agree to buy it, sight unseen. If she'll pay $150 for it, well, it's not a typical markup, but it's $50 that you didn't have before.

But it's also possible to find another knickknack made of purple slag buried in a box of junk at a yard sale. You offer the seller a couple of bucks for the box and if she's ignorant of the piece's real value, she says fine, just glad to have it off her hands. If you sell the vase at $150, you will have realized a markup of 7,500 percent. You could also let it go for less to a customer who does considerable business with you and you'll still come out way ahead.

The best way to price your merchandise is to always be aware of current selling prices. Because prices change daily, even hourly in some cases, it's important to stay on top of the fluctuations by reading as many antiques papers as you can get your hands on. This aspect of the business, of course, is another argument for specializing in only a few kinds of antiques. You'll have your hands full—you don't want to discourage customers with prices that are too high, but you don't want to let items go for much less than you're entitled to get for them, either.

And keep in mind that negotiating is a long lost art that is commonly practiced in the antiques business. If you like to dicker over prices with customers, you should then price your antiques and collectibles about 10 to 15 percent higher than you'd like to get. Some dealers hang hand-lettered signs throughout the shop that say, in effect, that negotiation is welcome so that customers won't feel that these artificially high prices are offensive or set in stone. If you don't like to dicker with your customers, you can set your prices at the actual levels you'd like to get for them, which should be in line with the current market value. But I'd advise against hanging up a sign in your shop that tells customers your prices are not negotiable. Signs that say No Dickering send a negative message to your customers and that is one thing that you don't need.

While you can get a realistic idea of how to price your merchandise by researching price guides and seeing what others ask for similar items, many dealers feel that the most realistic gauge of pricing comes from auctions. It's a good indicator of what people are willing to pay. While some dealers might automatically slice 10 to 15 percent off the price of a similar piece sold at auction to arrive at their shop or booth price, accounting for the bidding frenzy that often drives up the price of an item, some items actually sell well below their estimated value, especially when the bidding is less than spirited.

Price guides present a reality that is good only for the day that the book is published. Obsolescence quickly sets in, though a variety of circumstances will necessarily dictate a wide range of acceptable prices for a particular object.

In the end, however, after you digest all of the information you can gather, it still comes down to gut instinct and what you believe the market will bear.

Accounting Basics

In the daily routine of running your antiques business, you'll need to keep track of revenue coming in and expenses going out. You should set up an accounting system that works best for you and your business.

There are two kinds of accounting you can use to track revenue and expenses. One, *cash accounting*, involves simple bookkeeping where income is recorded when it is received, and expenses are recorded when they are paid, even if the expense was incurred in a different month. For instance, say a customer charges $300 worth of your merchandise to a credit card on the last day of a month. You put the charge through to the credit card, but the income is not posted in your account until a few days later, which happens to fall in the following month. With cash accounting, you will record the $300 in the month when you received it, even though you made the sale the previous month. This may give you an inaccurate picture of your business cycles. Cash accounting, however, is a very simple way to keep your books, and if you want to keep your business small and part-time, you might prefer its simplicity. You probably don't need an exact picture of your month-to-month revenue and expenses.

Accrual accounting is more painstaking in its execution, but it will provide you with a more accurate view of your revenue and expenses and the status of your financial situation each month. Even though payment may be received or credited the following month and expenses paid on a net-30 system, they are recorded in the current month's ledgers, when incurred and not actually paid or received.

When drawing up your accounting sheets, no matter which method you choose, refer to the categories named in the previous section, Estimating Operating Costs. You may want to list certain expenses in categories that are even more specific. Again, bear in mind the method and categories that will work best for your antiques business.

Your Daily Tasks

Running an antiques business, like any small business, demands that you learn to juggle several tasks at once and be able to switch back and forth between each of them suddenly, especially if you offer a variety of services to your customer base. For instance, one minute you may be ringing up a sale for a walk-in customer and the next the phone might ring with a call from a picker with a bargain on an item for which you've been looking. Then, while you're checking your records to see if you can afford it now, an overseas customer calls and asks you to conduct a search for her. If you are unable to switch gears quickly, you should think about putting somebody else in charge of certain tasks.

Undoubtedly, you'll be called on to perform a variety of tasks in the course of running your antiques business. Some of the duties, however, won't be necessary for you to do each day; sometimes certain tasks get bunched up all on one day or during a certain period of the month or year. It's up to you to be prepared to handle them—or have someone else who can. And once you've run your antiques business for a while, you'll start to develop a feel for the rhythm of the business and actually be able to anticipate some of the necessary tasks before they reach the "immediate attention requested" stage.

Hiring Employees

Some antiques business owners prefer to keep their operations small, specifically so they'll be able to handle all the jobs themselves without having to hire outside help. Hiring and managing employees adds a whole new dimension to your business and has both its good and bad points: For one, it means more paperwork because you'll have to pay state, federal, and perhaps local payroll taxes in addition to Social Security and worker's compensation and, if you decide to offer it, health insurance. On the other hand, having someone around to help out with the grunt work means you'll have more time to focus on running and building your business.

But unfortunately, a common complaint of business owners everywhere today is that it's hard to find good help; after all, no paid employee is going to regard your business and customers in the same meticulous and painstaking light that you will. So you'll probably have to lower your standards of quality and attention and plan to spend some time making up for the lack.

Many experienced antiques business owners suggest that if you find an employee who is the exception to the rule, hold onto them as tightly as you can by increasing pay, offering bonuses, and expressing your appreciation with added responsibilities along with an occasional day off with pay.

When hiring employees, there are certain things you must know. If you're hiring a person to work for you regularly, selling to customers, answering the phone or ringing up sales, that person will be considered to be your employee and you will have to withhold income taxes, which you will file with the government either quarterly or once a year, depending on your tax setup.

Some businesses get around the process of withholding and payroll taxes by hiring an employee as an independent contractor. This way, the contractor files a self-employment tax, which saves you a lot of paperwork. This works for such businesses that often hire seasonal and periodic help, but it will send up red flags about your business with the IRS if you try to hire a part-time employee in this way. The IRS has strict criteria for distinguishing an independent contractor from an employee, and this has been an area of abuse in small business. If you do hire an independent contractor and pay them more than $600 over the course of a year, you must file a 1099 form on their behalf which reports their income to the IRS.

No matter how you decide to staff your business, make sure that you always communicate clearly, directly, and immediately when there's a problem or complaint. And let people know when you think they did a job well.

Working with Suppliers

When you're first starting out, you'll probably buy the supplies you need to run your business—stationery, office equipment, and bags and boxes—from stores and businesses you have dealt with in the past. Later on, as you grow, you might want to deal directly with wholesalers and commercial distributors.

The first issue you'll face when approaching suppliers is meeting the large minimum orders they usually require to keep their costs down. Their minimum might be more than you'll use in a month—or a year—and you may not want to tie that much money up in office supplies when you'll probably need cash for other things. And when you check a supplier's prices, you might actually discover they're higher than what you'd pay in a retail store, since they include the cost of delivery and overhead. Even if you contact a distributor that deals in more than one type of supply, your combined potential order might be too small.

For many of the supplies you'll need to run your business, your best bet is to stick to your area businesses that you already know—and that know you. Many local businesses will allow you to set up a business charge account with them to simplify your bookkeeping. Some of these "suppliers" will also offer you a discount for buying in quantity and also for paying before 30 days.

Even if you buy retail, however, it still pays to shop around. When buying office supplies, for instance, you'll probably spend the most at your neighborhood stationery store. The next cheapest source will be a stationery superstore, though sometimes the quality and attention you'll receive is far below what you're used to. In my experience, the cheapest source of office supplies are the mail-order operations that ship the same day your order is received and offer large discounts on top of their already low prices for volume orders.

There are exceptions to everything, however, so the best advice is to take your time, shop around, and don't be afraid to dicker. These companies want your business, and if you show you're going to be a good, steady customer, they'll work hard to keep you.

Understanding Taxes

When you first set up your antiques business and discover how much time, energy, and paperwork you have to spend on taxes, you might wonder when you'll find the time to do anything else. After payroll taxes, your income and other personal taxes, and the state sales tax, you may wonder why you should even bother. After all, why go into business if most of your revenue will go towards taxes?

Calm down. It only seems overwhelming now as you're learning about the different responsibilities of a business owner. Once you get the hang of it, recording and paying taxes—as well as figuring out your deductions—will consume just a small part of your bookkeeping and office time. As mentioned in the long run you'll save time if you keep good records.

Of course, you will need to keep track of your revenue and expenses and pay taxes to the IRS on any profit that your antiques business earns. The amount of tax you pay will depend on the type of business you're running: a sole proprietorship or partnership, or a corporation. The tax structures for each differ.

Of course, since the start-up costs for your antiques business will consume most of your revenue for the first year or two, your expenses may even exceed your revenue, negating the need to pay tax. The IRS allows that there will be years when you'll earn no profit on paper, even though it assumes you are in business to earn a profit. As a result, many businesses claim a wealth of deductions to avoid showing a profit, and therefore, paying tax. Current tax law says that you must show a profit at least three years out of five to prove that you are running a viable business. If you show a loss three or more years out of the five, this will alert the IRS and set you up for the possibility of an audit.

As for payroll taxes, contact your state employment bureau about the exact deductions you should make for each employee, in addition to the federal tax bureau for information about income tax, Social Security, and other payroll taxes.

Spotlight

Depression Glass

Depression glass is one of the most popular types of antiques. But even though the low prices of many pieces allow a collector to start building a sizable collection right away, the prices of some Depression glass pieces can run into the hundreds of dollars and will only continue to appreciate in value.

Many collectors actually use Depression glass as their everyday dishware; indeed, it offers an elegance and style that you can't readily find in most of the dishware being produced today. And the cost of most of the Depression glass that's out there is surprisingly not much more than a new set of dishes.

Manufactured by a variety of companies, Depression glass hails from the 1920s through the 1950s, comes in pale shades of pink, yellow, and green. Later glass from the 1940s and 1950s tends to be in bolder, brighter colors, like ultramarine and cobalt blue. Indeed, the prices of Depression glass are largely based on the manufacturers and the type of dish. Butter dishes, cookie jars, and pitchers tend to bring the highest prices.

It's possible to find Depression glass plates and cups in certain styles that sell for under $10 a piece. But be careful of buying reproductions instead of the real thing; you can detect reproductions by their distinctive colors. Any of the ten price guides that are published on Depression glass can alert you to the original colors for each piece. Look for these books in bookstores or check *Books in Print* at your local library.

Action Guidelines

✔ Estimate in advance what it will cost each month to run your antiques business.

✔ Develop a system that painlessly allows you to maintain accurate records.

✔ Set the prices for your items according to instinct and what the market will bear.

✔ Pick cash accounting or accrual accounting as a way to set up your books.

✔ Be clear about the pros and cons about hiring employees for your antiques business.

MARKETING

For many antiques business owners, the term *marketing* is enough to conjure up fear and loathing. Why? Because the idea of selling yourself or your business makes many people uncomfortable. Marketing may bring to mind images of slick, expensive ad campaigns as well as the feeling that there's something mystical about the ability to draw in customers on the strength of just your words or pictures.

Contrary to popular belief, you don't need a degree in marketing in order to sell your business effectively. In fact, you're actually the ideal person to market your own business and will do it better than a professional, simply because you know your business best. And because both your funds and time are limited when you're first starting out, you'll probably have to rely more heavily on creativity than someone who has a degree in marketing and unlimited funds. And in marketing any small business, it's creativity that counts.

Even so, if you're thinking of hiring somebody else to do your marketing just to get the job off your hands, forget about it. Just as no one else will know your customers like you do, likewise you are the best person to promote your antiques business. After all, who else is better acquainted with the business and therefore better able to convey its value to others?

By the time you finish reading this chapter, you may grudgingly start to admit that marketing can actually be fun and as creative as arranging a store display. Again, the more creative you are, the better—for you and your antiques business.

The Purpose of Marketing

You already know that you have a great product: your antiques business, whatever its form. But how will anyone hear about it unless you let them know you exist?

"Oh, they'll see the sign out front or my ad in the weekly paper," you'll reply. As with any ad or notice that promotes your antiques business, it's a fact that only a tiny percentage of the people who pass by your shop or see your ad will respond by coming in and buying something from you.

"Well, what about the chamber of commerce? I'm a member, you know." Yes, and so are 300 other businesses in your town, all seeking the same thing you are—more customers.

Joining the chamber of commerce, a regional antiques dealers association, or another local business organization is a great idea, but you should realize that there are limits to what they can do for you. After all, their role is to promote area businesses as a group to attract shoppers to your area, not to market each business individually.

"My brochure really knocks 'em dead." Great, but how are you going to get it in the hands of prospective customers in the first place? It's a benefit if your brochure and other promotional materials manage to convey in an exciting way what customers can expect from your business. However, you must distribute it—through your own customer list, by dropping off copies at local businesses, or by other means.

The purpose of marketing is to develop and execute a number of different strategies that increase your exposure and sales. Admittedly, some customers will stumble upon your business. One important marketing task that you can do is to always make sure that your shop or booth is inviting to passersby. This is the only way to market to potential customers who come in by accident.

To cultivate more planned business, however, you must devote time and creativity to the marketing plan that you developed in Chapter Four. Always keep in mind that marketing, in whatever form, will help you to meet new customers—and then bring them back. Repeat business is the lifeblood of any antiques business; and the best thing about repeat customers, besides the friendships you'll cultivate, is the fact that getting them back incurs little or no additional marketing costs. They're already convinced and you don't have to sell them on the merits of your antiques business and services.

Defining Your Customers

Your customers will encompass a large cross-section of the population: young, old, singles, couples, and families. And most of them are largely overwhelmed by the thousands of messages the media sends out each day. Therefore, the majority of the messages sent by small businesses have become quite specialized in addressing the target audience.

You must do the same thing. You won't be able to reach everybody within your target market and even if you could, because they are overwhelmed, chances are they won't notice it the first time out—or even the tenth. The first step to reaching your customers is to target the specific kind of customer that you'd like to attract, even though a wide variety will eventually do business with you over the years. Keeping individual records about your customers from the beginning—how they heard about your business, what kinds of items they buy and how often—can help you to define your customer even more once you've been in business for awhile.

Granted, the type of antiques business you run, the kinds of antiques and collectibles you offer, your location, and your pricing structure will largely determine the kinds of customers you will attract to your antiques business. Of course, there will be exceptions, but generally, the best thing you should do is to first define your ideal customer and then let the rest discover your business as part of the wide marketing net you'll cast.

The advantage of defining your ideal customer is that you can then narrow down your choice of the ways you have to reach them, as well as the methods you'll use.

Record in your notebook your answers to the following questions:

1. What are the three types of customers you'd like to reach? For example, people who buy big-ticket items once a year, those who come in regularly to browse to see what's recently come in, or people with money who want to remain faceless and deal with your solely through the mail?

2. Where do they live, within a 10-mile radius of your shop or hundreds of miles away?

3. What is their income range? Are they urban professionals with discretionary income or casual shoppers looking for a bargain?

4. Why will they do business with you?

5. What will they spend, on average, with you during each visit or order?

Finding Prospects

You have a picture of your ideal customer, as well as other types of people who will do business with you. Now, how do you find them?

Through a variety of ways. You should know, however, that prospects are not the same thing as customers. In fact, only a small percentage of people who inquire about the antiques you have for sale, walk by your booth at a show or mall, or see your brochure will actually make a purchase from you. You must, however, view all prospects as potential customers, and treat them with the kind of respect that you'd demand. But don't show your disappointment or make a comment when they walk by without buying something. America is full of what I call fishermen: because there is so much out there to choose from, we must know all there is about everything there is before we make a decision. And even then, there's a little voice in the back of our heads that says, "There's always something better." So many people end up not doing anything as a result, forever stuck in their indecision.

Perhaps it is true that there is "always something better." But you can help find and convert more of your prospects into paying customers by focusing your marketing efforts on those avenues that your ideal customer regularly travels. For instance, is she a serious collector, scanning a particular regional antiques newspaper for auction news and prices each month? Then you should take out an ad in each issue in order to reach her.

Are you expanding your business in order to carry other types of items, or have you recently purchased a mint condition piece that's quite rare? Send a news release to the antiques publications and the business or lifestyle editor of your local daily paper for a shot at an interview or profile of your business.

Do you want to target customers who live in a major city two hours away and who travel to your area every month or so? Then spend a couple days in the city, distributing brochures, doing radio and TV talk shows and newspaper interviews. Contact and meet with the director of a local woman's club or some other social group a few weeks in advance and do a luncheon talk about what it's like to operate an antiques business. At the end, pass out your brochure and discount coupons inviting members of the audience to visit your antiques business sometime within the next month.

Got the idea? Marketing is not always advertising, as many people wrongly assume. In fact, advertising is one of the least effective and most expensive ways to locate and develop your prospects.

Think about your defined customers and then consider the places you'll be able to find them; use some of the above suggestions for a jumping-off point. You'll undoubtedly be able to think of many more.

Cloning and Keeping Good Customers

Once you get a good customer, hold onto him or her. Tight. The good news is that your good customer knows other people who could also be good customers. After all, word of mouth is probably the most effective kind of marketing there is.

There are a variety of ways you can clone good customers. One way—if you send a regular letter, price list, or note about your new acquisitions to regular customers—is to ask them if they know of other people who would like to receive this privileged information. Keep track of any reservations you receive through this referral system; you can then offer discounts to customers who refer others to you.

If you offer a search service to customers as part of your business, you'll probably pick up the phone to call them when a new item that they've been looking for comes in. You might also want to do this with other items you think they might like. It's important to gauge their reactions, however. Some customers may be delighted that you think of them; others may think that your calls are an intrusion.

If you treat your regular customers well with every contact, you are cloning good customers in the best way possible, since they are likely to come back again and again.

Some antiques businesses report that more than 50 percent of their business comes from customers who buy from them regularly. The best way to build up to this level and continue to clone other good customers is to continue to market to your targeted group of customers, and be consistent in maintaining the quality of your antiques business and the items you sell. After all, one of the reasons why customers will continue to do business with you is because they know what to expect.

Finding the Time

Finding the time is one of the biggest problems that antiques business owners say they have when it comes to marketing. If you block out periods of time to market, or just keep the idea of marketing in the forefront—like having some ideas spread out on the counter so you can write some ads or work on your press kit when there are no customers in the store—it's all but impossible to ignore it.

Here are some ideas you can follow whenever you complain that you lack the time to market.

- A lot of marketing involves grunt work: stuffing envelopes, making lists, shuffling through ad rate cards. Do this during slow times of the day or night; it's easier to justify when ten other things aren't demanding your attention.

- Examine your slow times, whether it's every Monday or the month of March. Use it to write your marketing plan, setting up the following year's strategies (see Chapter 4). Then perform maintenance tasks on your weekly slow day.

- Survey your staff for ideas. If appropriate, let them carry them out with your approval. Pay for all expenses, and hold a monthly contest for the best idea. They may surprise you.

- Here's a sneaky tip: Ask sales reps from different media to design a media plan for you as a way to get your business. Many reps will do this anyway, of course, giving the biggest percentage of the pie to themselves. Whether you follow through is up to you, but you'll get lots of suggestions and ideas at no cost or time spent.

Always ask about upcoming promotional tie-in events; frequently you'll get a reduced rate and increased exposure at the event as well.

- Hire someone to carry out your plan if you truly can't find enough time, or give the responsibility to a staff member. One outfitter hired a PR consultant who was just starting out. She paid the consultant a below-market rate but tied bonuses into any increased business that resulted from the additional publicity. Some times novices are better than experts; although they don't have the contacts, they also don't have a lot of preconceived notions about what's right and what's wrong. With marketing, innovation gets attention.

Advertising on a Budget

With advertising you pay for a certain amount of space or time so you can tell your message to a particular audience. Since you're paying to send the message, you can say anything you want—time or space and money are the only factors that limit you.

Considering these limitations, advertising doesn't really give you much leeway. In fact, because you bought the space, you're obviously selling something and the majority of people turn right off when someone's trying to sell them something.

Take a look at the ads in your local newspaper or magazine. What do they look like? How do they make you feel? Is there one that makes you want to drop what you're doing, pick up the phone and call?

Probably not. Do the same thing the next time you're watching TV or listening to the radio. Pay close attention to the locally produced ads. Again, do they make you feel excited about whatever it is the advertiser is trying to sell?

I probably can predict what your answer will be. The vast majority of advertising in all media is placed to gain consumer awareness, to let people know that a business exists. And this type of advertising can build business for your antiques business—but very slowly—and it should be considered as only one part of a successful marketing campaign, not the entire program. Also, the results from advertising are sometimes hard to measure. How often do you go into a store and say that you saw their ad in the newspaper unless you're specifically doing so to get a discount unless the owner is a friend of yours? Probably not very often.

Because advertising is so expensive, you can't waste money to use it just to let people know you're there. Publicity and other more direct marketing tools exist for this reason and they're cheap.

No, the primary reasons why you should spend money to advertise is to support a special promotion or discount available for a limited time; or to offer something to customers who respond to your ad. A toll-free number, a discount coupon, or a special incentive will help you measure how many people responded and purchased something from you as the direct result of your ad. Then you can see if the ad paid for itself and whether you should try another ad again later. And if the ad is inexpensive, as they tend to be in the regional antiques trade newspapers, go ahead and try an ad, but order at least three continued insertions and preferably more. As I've said, most people don't respond the first time they see your ad. Once they become familiar with you, more of them will tend to check you out. Some antiques businesses might think that the following suggestion is tacky, but I still feel the best way to measure your ad response is to tell readers to mention the ad or bring it in for a special deal. In addition to being able to track your ad response, you'll probably also attract more customers, since you're offering them something that most other advertisers aren't.

Some antiques business owners report that they've felt pressure from a newspaper or magazine editor to advertise in exchange for a promise to cover their business in an editorial section of the publication. Though most editors will deny this ever happens, I can tell you from experience that it does; but it's most likely to occur at smaller publications, where most or all of their revenue comes from advertising. And when the publisher also serves as the editor, you can be sure that any conflict of interest between advertising and editorial departments frequently will be ignored.

If you do decide to advertise, never settle for the quoted rate. Always ask, "Is that the best you can do?" Especially if the publication is nearing its closing date and there's still ad space left to fill, the sales rep or ad director might let it go at a significant discount. In addition, some publications frequently offer a special rate to first-time advertisers in the hopes that they'll become regular advertisers. At other times, they'll offer a discount if you advertise in a special section or sponsor a certain program. Again, you should always ask.

Radio and TV advertising don't usually work for antiques businesses, since it is a very expensive and broad medium for you to reach your very small target audience. It's best to focus on print ads in antiques publications and other magazines and newspapers that your target audience reads regularly.

Publicity

There are many antiques business owners who think that publicity is the best kind of marketing around since, aside from the initial costs of preparing a press release and contacting the media about your antiques business, publicity is free. And because, when your business receives coverage in a magazine or newspaper, on radio, or TV, you can consider it a direct and effective endorsement of your business. You didn't have to pay to get mentioned and the audience naturally responds more favorably to an unsolicited endorsement than to a paid ad.

As with defining your customer, you must also narrow down the media you wish to reach. Many times, your ideal customer will select your media for you. For instance, if your ideal guest has a professional career, collects antiques as a hobby, and lives in a large city two hours from your antiques business but has a summer home in your area, you might target urban magazines and the magazines in the Sunday newspapers that regularly cover antiques. Best Buys section will often mention unusual finds and usually, these types of businesses don't necessarily have to be within the city limits. To determine to whom to send your information, you should check the masthead for the name of one of the editors, or use the name of the writer who regularly handles stories on antiques and collectibles. Never contact the editor-in-chief of a large or frequent publication, since they will be far too busy to respond to you. The managing editor or an associate editor is a far better choice.

In any case, you will need to send the editor or writer a copy of your brochure, any other promotional materials, price lists, copies of other stories that have been written about your antiques business, and a cover letter and press release.

A cover letter should be short and to the point, and casual in tone. It also helps if you show you're familiar with the publication and the writer's work by mentioning a recent story. Try to highlight one thing that makes your antiques business different from others in the area. After all, the editor probably gets bombarded with mailings from all types of businesses every day; his attitude about yours is probably going to be, "So what?"

Figure 7.1, on p. 140, is one sample cover letter. Adapt it to fit your needs.

It's also a good idea to offer an angle for a story. Note that the owner of Wildflower Antiques didn't specifically ask that the editor write a story about his business. This appeals to editors and writers who frequently get letters that are quite pushy from people who desperately want to be written up. Your laid-back attitude will easily win you brownie points with editors and writers.

Dear Editor:

I own an antiques shop called Wildflower Antiques in Agawam, Massachusetts. Enclosed is a brochure and an article that the local paper published about our extensive collection of primitive farm tools.

I thought you'd like to know about Wildflower Antiques, since I read your recent article about the Weed Antiques Shop, which is one hour south of Boston. We're two hours west.

The next time you're planning a story on this area or on how people in Boston are decorating their homes with primitive farm tools, give me a call. I could pass along the names of several of my customers in Boston for you to talk to. I'd also be glad to fill you in on some of the other interesting antiques shops in town.

Sincerely,

Tom Wildflower

Figure 7.1: Publicity Cover Letter

Promotional Materials

Your brochure is the most important part of your marketing arsenal. Many times, it will be the first impression that a prospective guest has about your antiques business. As such, it has the potential to make or break your business. And once you're set on the design for your brochure, all of your other promotional materials—stationery and business cards—should follow the same theme and look.

Basically, your brochure should consist of these seven ingredients:

1. A description of your antiques business
2. A map and directions
3. A detailed description of your offerings
4. A photograph or line drawing of some of your antiques and collectibles
5. Your background in the antiques and collectibles field
6. Your name, address, and phone number and fax if applicable
7. A current price list

It's a good idea to print the price list on a separate sheet of paper to insert into the body of the brochure. With a separate price list, this allows you to include last-minute arrivals as well as discounts on items that made your last price list but haven't yet sold. It also saves money—by printing a large run of 5,000 or 10,000 brochures you'll pay less per brochure and can accommodate later price changes with your insert. You can also distribute the brochure around town, where there's no need to include a price list. This quantity of brochures could last several years, depending upon your business and area.

The style of your brochure is up to you. Most small antiques businesses, however, have brochures that tend to be quite simple, with one color of ink on an 8½ by 11-inch piece of textured ivory or cream-colored paper folded into three panels. I don't think you'll need glossy brochures with a number of four-color photos to attract customers to your store. Keep it simple and you'll tend to attract more of the people who collect antiques specifically for the simplicity they represent.

Beyond Your Traditional Markets

When you start your antiques business, it will take some time to develop a steady customer base. You'll reach people who see your shop, pick up your brochure, respond to your ad, or see an article about you and your business in the local paper. When a customer discovers you through untraditional channels and then makes a purchase and turns into a regular customer, it can almost seem like found money.

Great, you think, I'm having enough trouble finding the time to do marketing at all and now I have to go hunting for business in *other* places as well?

Don't worry; these other places are just as easy and inexpensive to pursue. In fact, they're even cheaper than the traditional outlets and tend to bring you a higher rate of return on your investment of time and money simply because most other antiques businesses don't even know enough to go after them. So by default, not to mention the kind of antiques and collectibles you carry, you'll be the standout.

Here they are. And don't be shy.

1. *Donate your space or a one-day outing to local nonprofit groups.* Frequently, nonprofit groups will need to host special events, like informational meetings or cocktail parties for their current and prospective members and contributors. If you offer the use of your space, it will not only help out the group but will also serve as an open house of sorts for you. These groups and their contributors tend to remember largesse, and it'll cost you next to nothing for them to use the space.

2. *Church groups and women's clubs are always looking for speakers for monthly meetings; volunteer!* Your best bet is to arrange to speak at a club luncheon in a city that tends to bring you lots of business. The topic? What it's like to be in the antiques business, which, as you know, is a business that many people dream about. Hand out your brochure and price list with your personal invitation for them to visit.

3. *Canvass the engagement notices in the newspaper every week.* Some might think this practice to be comparable to reading the obits in a city where good apartments are at a premium, but it's a great idea if you want wedding business. If you have the inventory, you can send a personalized letter offering a bridal registry service for the guests of the bride and groom. If they take you up on your registry, send the couple a gift on their first anniversary.

4. *Advertise in a place where you've never seen a business like yours advertise before.* But make it a classified with a knockout headline. Two places that come to mind are the back pages of the Boston *Phoenix* and New York's *Village Voice*, which are nothing *but* classified ads. Promote an offer that is almost impossible for antiques and collectibles buffs to refuse. You might want to use these ads to develop your mail-order business and to offer certain collectibles—like '60s and '70s memorabilia—that specifically applies to this audience.

5. *Don't overlook group tour operators.* I can tell you in advance that this can be a tough nut to crack. However, once you're in and a regularly-scheduled part of the tour, your reputation and bottom line will grow. Group tour operators run mostly extended bus tours; however, some tours can last a day or less and be geared towards locals and not tourists. If you can convince the operator to include you as a regular stop on the tour—historical tours are more likely to be interested for obvious reasons—especially as the last stop, then the tour partici-

pants will take the time to browse and possibly buy from you. It's always a good idea to offer free refreshments, to encourage and lengthen the amount of time they spend in your shop. To make initial contact with a bus tour company, you should first call the operator's office and ask for a catalog to get an idea of the focus of their tours. Find out where the operator's current tours run, how far away from your shop they operate, and what their target market is. Ask if they're planning to expand to other areas in the future. Offer to serve as their contact for your area. Keep in touch, and regularly send them news of new services and attractions in your area. Suggest itineraries; send maps and brochures.

Another sideline is to make friends with your local step-on guides as a way to reach the operators. Step-on guides are hired by the tour operator to provide an in-depth tour of a locale; they are particularly valued for niche or historical tours, which is a benefit for you. If you don't know who they are, contact your local chamber of commerce or tourist association for names and numbers.

Spotlight

Pez Dispensers

The best antique or collectible that anyone could specialize in is the kind that makes them smile. For me, even though they aren't technically antiques, it's Pez dispensers. In fact, although Pez dispensers have now been manufactured for several decades, whenever I'm in line at the local discount department store, I always crane my neck to see what kinds of new Pez dispensers are on sale.

Pez dispensers seem to have become a microcosm of popular culture in America over the years—Disney characters appear on top of some, as well as a whole slew of familiar faces from the Merrie Melodie cartoons.

Like many newer collectibles from the '60s and '70s, Pez dispensers have only become popular since the early 1990s. Fortunately, they're still relatively inexpensive to collect. The most expensive Pez dispenser I've seen is a Popeye model that sold for $40 in 1994. Most, however, range from $6 to around $20, though these prices are bound to rise.

For some reason, like the new Pez dispensers, the Pez candy today just isn't what it used to be. I guess childhood sharpens your senses for everything while adulthood dulls them, so that it takes something like an object of absolute whimsy from your childhood to spark those senses up again.

Action Guidelines

✔ Analyze the types of customers you'd like to reach.

✔ Think about the places you're most likely to find them.

✔ Continually market to customers who have already bought an item from you at least once.

✔ Don't consider advertising to be your only form of marketing.

✔ Be cordial but not overly fawning when dealing with the press.

Profile

Bruce Magowan
Antique Mall Exhibitor
Quechee, Vermont

In 1987, Bruce Magowan and his wife, Gail, bought a large Victorian house in Bordentown, New Jersey. She started filling it with antiques to such an extent that one day Bruce told her she'd have to start selling some of them. At the time, he owned a men's clothing shop. He offered to turn over some shelf space in the store to Gail for the antiques. She called it— what else?—The Shelf.

A few years later, he sold the clothing store and opened an antiques shop, which didn't pan out, so he decided to go into a coop space where all he had to do was stock it.

Then he found Timber Village, a cooperative antique mall on a busy highway in Quechee, Vermont. He started renting a five-foot booth space in 1981. "I stock it, they sell it, and they send me a check every two weeks," he says. "The people are good to work with, over a million customers walk through the mall each year, and it's open 364 days a year. Plus, it gives me a chance to go to Vermont."

The Magowans still buy from their travels, though Bruce admits it's more of a fun thing than a major boost to their income. The rental costs $72 a month; he grosses about $400 a month. He restocks the booth every other month. His specialty is small objects, especially matchsafes, of which he has an extensive collection.

Matchsafes are small containers that hung by the wood or coal cookstove in the kitchen at the turn of the century. Some had one cup to hold unused matches, others had two, one of which held the used ones. They were made from tin, brass, or leather, and some were giveaways from coal companies. Bruce also has a collection of "what-do-you-call-these-things." His collection attracts the attention of many people who want to puzzle it out; they often end up buying it.

Bruce tags each item with the name and the price. The purchaser brings items to a main counter near the front of the store where the cashier records the sale.

"I put in about five hours a week. Some weeks, I'll spend more time," he reports. "I also travel around looking for antiques. I go to shops, auctions, and big antique shows."

He tries to be discriminating in the items he buys. "There's a lot of junk out there; there's stuff from the '50s and '60s that I don't consider to be antiques. I try to go much older." He suggests a person who's interested in starting up a booth in an antique mall seek the advice of someone who knows the business. "A good friend took me out a long time ago and showed me what to look for and what not to look for," he recalls. "I still go back to him and ask for advice on prices. You could be in this business for a lifetime and still not know all the answers."

When they visit Vermont to restock the booth, they stay in a motel room. Bruce's dream is to buy a house in Vermont with an attached garage and a barn where he could open another antique shop. "When my wife retires," he says, "I'll do it."

Chapter
8

FINANCES

Finances are just about the only part of the antiques business that is pretty cut and dry; that is, how to keep track of the finances in your business. The other financial part of your business—setting prices and buying and selling antiques—lies on the other side of the pendulum swing and will probably be the most unpredictable part of your business.

As with the other necessary things you have to do in order to get your business off the ground, the issue of dealing with your finances certainly isn't the most important part of your business, but without it, you'll be constantly skirting an invitation to join the Failed Business Club.

Profits and Losses

One of the best ways to keep track of how your business is doing is to prepare a profit and loss statement. Even though money may be coming in regularly through the sales of your antiques and the other services you offer, you may actually be losing money because your expenses exceed your income.

Keeping good records will help make preparing a profit and loss statement that much easier; all you have to do is plug in the numbers. There are two kinds of profit and loss statements you can keep: one that projects your estimated profits and losses and another that tracks actual figures on a weekly or monthly basis to help you see how well your antiques business is doing. You can also compare the two and if your projections are either 20 percent higher or lower than your actual figures, based on seasonality, you can adjust your projected profit and loss statements accordingly.

With an antiques business that you operate out of your home, it may be difficult to accurately figure your expenses, since some of your own personal expenses, like the mortgage and your utilities, will overlap into your business expenses. That's why it's always a good idea to set aside one room in your home for your business and use it for no other purpose, for the sake of your own record keeping and also to keep the IRS at bay.

To figure out your profit and loss statement for your antiques business, you must first add up your gross revenues, which is every dollar that your antiques business brings in over the course of the year. Then get out the list of operating costs you drew up in Chapter Six and again, using either actual figures or estimates, add all of your expenses for the year. You'll include salaries, the mortgage and utilities, business loans, office expenses, buying antiques and collectibles, everything.

And don't forget about depreciation. Ask your accountant for advice on this, but chances are that you'll be able to deduct the amount that is deemed to depreciate on your house, office equipment, and other big-ticket items you bought for your business this year. This is not strictly an expense but will serve to help lower your profit, which will then lower your tax bill.

Don't forget about the interest you pay on any loans connected with the business. And remember that the type of business you run—sole proprietorship, partnership, or corporation—also will affect your profit and loss statement.

After deducting all of your expenses from your revenue, you'll be left with a pretax profit or loss. There's one more step, though. Now deduct all of the taxes you pay in connection with your business—except payroll taxes, which are figured into your payroll expenses—and you will come up with your actual net profit or loss, which probably seems a long way from your initial gross revenue figure.

Running a small antiques business probably won't be a huge money-maker for you, at least in the beginning; but for most people that's not the point. Your business may have grossed $24,000, but with $18,000 in expenses, your profit will come to $6,000, which is your taxable income. Though you'll always have certain fixed expenses, there are a variety of ways you can adjust your profit or loss: reducing your expenses, raising your prices, buying merchandise for less, and increasing your marketing and exposure are just a few. Over time, you will be able to see which items cultivate repeat business and which don't. Running an antiques business is a constant experiment as well as a source of joy. Your profit and loss statement is a reminder of how well your experiment is doing.

Keeping Track of Your Money

Most antiques business owners use a variety of methods to help them keep track of their money, both revenue and expenses.

The basic record will probably be your checkbook. There are a number of business checking accounts that come with built-in ledgers where you can record your expenses under different expense categories at the same time you write a check. Separating these expenses in advance makes it easy at the end of the year to determine how much you've spent in each category, and if you need to cut back.

Some antiques businesses prefer to keep their financial records on computer. Software can keep track of your expenses and income, categorize them, add them up in a flash, and even print out checks.

To keep track of your revenue, you should keep a record of each sale you make, either in writing or on computer. Any software program that combines a database with a spreadsheet will serve you well. You might also want some other features like word processing and mailing list programs that will allow you to merge the names of your customer list with the word processing program for customized letters and mailing lists. Whatever method you choose, make sure that it's easy to use and that you check in with it at least once a week. Letting it go for any longer than that will make keeping track of your money a chore and something you're likely to put off; and you'll be more likely to make mistakes.

Fortunately, some of the companies that you'll do business with are making it easier for their customers to keep track of their money. Credit and charge card companies now offer a breakdown of charges in different categories on their monthly statement. Some of the suppliers with which you maintain an account also will provide this service. And if they don't, ask. They might start.

Developing Your Credit

If you're in business for any length of time, you're going to need credit in one form or another. Most of the time, it will be from suppliers who deal with you on a regular basis and who don't deal in picking up cash or checks with each delivery. Not only is it too unwieldy and increases the possibility of loss, it's a big waste of time.

But most suppliers and other companies won't offer you credit unless you've done business with them before. It's the old Catch 22—how can you develop your credit if no one will give you any in the first place?

Fortunately, there are ways around this. Many companies will open a credit line for you based on your personal credit record. They'll usually start you out small and then increase your credit line as your history with them grows. Needless to say, you'll help your credit line if you always pay promptly, even before the due date—and by acting promptly whenever there is a question about your account.

With other suppliers, you'll need to prove yourself in the beginning and your personal credit, no matter how stellar, will have nothing to do with it. These companies will make you pay cash or by check before they deliver the goods; only after a certain period of time will they begin to extend you credit, and only a little at a time.

Once you begin to establish a credit record with your antiques business, you'll undoubtedly be solicited by charge card companies that invite you to open a business account with a high credit limit and low monthly payments. Though having a business credit card account helps in many instances—such as renting a car or buying airline tickets in certain situations—try not to use them too much. Because cards are almost universally accepted—even the IRS takes MasterCard and Visa now—and it's easier to slap down the plastic than to apply for a basic account with a supplier, you might be tempted to run up huge bills with their inherent high interest charges. This is a high price to pay for apparent convenience. Instead, use them sparingly, appreciate them for what they are—an extremely expensive way to borrow money—and be as judicious with their use and payment as you are with your other creditors. After all, they can help develop your credit rating, too.

Although banks are a lot pickier now about lending money even to people with unblemished credit ratings, you might apply for a line of credit at your bank, if you don't have one already. Learning to rely on it only in emergency financial situations, then paying back the money as soon as possible will help your business get through the tough times, which you will certainly have.

Working with Suppliers

As I've already said, one part of working with suppliers is to build up credit, and a working relationship. There are other ways as well.

Getting the best price may be the most important thing to you. Other antiques business owners might be attracted by a company's frequent delivery schedule, while still others might favor a particular business because of the brands that supplier offers.

Most suppliers will bend over backwards to get your business, though you may find that you'll have to jump through a few hoops at first, for instance, to get a credit account set up in your initial dealings with the company.

There are many ways to find the suppliers who will work with you and who you'll feel most comfortable working with. You should know if one supplier doesn't give you the terms you'd like, there are others who will. Don't sign on with one right away—take the time to shop around for the best price, the quality you want, and the working relationship you feel comfortable with. Whether you prefer to deal by mail and have the items delivered to your door or pick them up yourself, it's easy to find the best supplier for your antiques business, from stationery to paper bags imprinted with your name and even special light bulbs for your display cases.

Borrowing Money

The issue of borrowing money in these credit-weary days is apt to be a sticky one among aspiring antiques business owners who may have to take out a second mortgage to buy an existing antiques shop or start one from scratch, or else in order to build up your inventory. "I'm in enough debt already," you may say, "Why would I want to borrow any more?"

As you'll see in an upcoming section later in this chapter, sometimes your cash flow won't keep up with your expenses. Even if you or a partner holds down a steady job, trust me when I say there will be times when that won't be enough. Operating and maintaining an antiques business with constant overhead, along with the occasional piece that is still on your shelves after a year, will eat up cash that you probably can't spare. During those times, it may be necessary to borrow.

If you have a rich relative or a sizable trust fund, you can skip over this section. But if you're like most of us, you'll need to rely on a conventional financing source.

I know of many examples where antiques business owners have drawn on their credit cards to initially build up their inventories, paid them off, and then run them right back up when things get slow. At anywhere from a 12 to 21 percent annual rate of interest, relying on credit cards is an expensive way to borrow money. Even if you fully intend to pay the money back before the interest has a chance to significantly add up, there will be times—you know, since you've been through them before—when you are only able to make the minimum payment. And since you already know to anticipate these cycles, especially in a business that can be somewhat seasonal, you should take steps now to line up an available source of credit that you can draw upon immediately.

Some antiques business owners decide to form partnerships for this reason alone: to have a silent partner with deep pockets who's looking for a better rate of return on his money than the banks can offer. But if you prefer to have a partner for other reasons—or to go it alone—and you don't want to have to rely on your credit cards, there is another option, and that is to open a line of credit at your bank.

If you don't want to go this route—or get turned down—there is the old-fashioned way, and that is to save for a rainy day. When business is booming and revenue is strong, set aside a certain percentage—some recommend from 5 to 25 percent of your revenue—and stash it away in an interest-bearing savings account. But I wouldn't put it in an investment where you don't have instant access to your funds; even though the interest rate may be better, you'll probably pay more by paying a penalty or fees for withdrawal from an IRA, mutual fund, or other investment. A money market fund is best; the interest rates tends to be a little higher than a passbook savings account, and you have immediate access to your money.

How to Raise Additional Capital

Because the revenue from an antiques business can be sporadic at times, and you'll need to have cash on hand when a certain gotta-have-it item comes on the market, many antiques business owners regularly turn to other sources of income, whether it's offering additional services to their customers, finding another job, or relying on a spouse's income to pay the bills. Most entrepreneurs have to raise additional capital when they first start their businesses. Some people turn to parents or relatives, while others rely on the proceeds from the sale of their primary house and move to start their antiques business in an area where they can get a lot more house for their money. Still others decide to sell a few choice pieces from their collection in order to raise enough money to start up.

For most people who have mortgages and no other regular income, the best way to raise the additional capital needed to start an antiques business and then keep it afloat is to offer other products and services connected with your business that you can sell to your customers. You could sell books on antiques to customers in your shop, at shows, or through the mail. You could also offer your services as an appraiser, contract out repair work, and run local seminars for collectors. Some antiques dealers have taken to offering a guided historical tour and sightseeing service to customers and tourists who may then buy more of your antiques and collectibles.

You have to be creative to stay in business these days, no matter what your venture is. The advantage of other services that you offer is that many of them will result in additional customers for your antiques business, thus bringing your efforts full-circle.

How to Give Credit to Customers

The primary way that most businesses extend credit to their customers is by accepting major credit cards. MasterCard, Visa, American Express, Discover, and Diner's Club are accepted by many antiques businesses. The credit companies will charge a fee to set you up with their service and then you'll pay the credit company a percentage of every transaction made by a customer, usually two to five percent. Your account is typically credited within one to three days after you entered the transactions into the system and there are certain restrictions each company places on its members, depending on the amount your antiques business will gross, among other factors. It is relatively simple to apply for privileges that will allow you to accept credit cards from your patrons.

However, some antiques business owners decide not to accept charge cards from their customers. Either their volume is too low to justify paying the commissions, or else the credit company places too many restrictions on them. Some have also said that the companies tend to have a patronizing attitude toward smaller companies because small antiques businesses simply don't provide the commission revenue that larger businesses do.

Other owners just figure that if a customer wants something badly enough, he'll buy it whether he can pay for it with a credit card or a check. I've seen instances where people will decide not to eat at a particular restaurant because it doesn't accept credit cards and no one in the party has enough cash.

I also have heard about some antiques business owners who accept credit cards but will ask customers if they can instead pay by cash or check. Many customers agree without a fuss; either way, a sale has been gained. In some cases, the owner will give the customer a discount if they pay cash.

By accepting credit cards, you'll have more impulse buyers looking over your merchandise, whether in your shop or at an antiques shows. Say you have a booth at an antiques show. You and the man in the next booth over both have the same type of item, an old Tonka truck in mint condition. A customer comes along and sees the two Tonka trucks. Your neighbor takes MasterCard, Visa, and American Express. You don't. If the price is the same, and the customer doesn't have enough cash and still wants the truck, guess what he's going to do?

So even if you hate the idea of credit cards, you should definitely arrange to accept them. It may be money in someone else's pocket if you don't.

Another way to arrange for certain customers to have credit is to set up a house charge account for regular patrons. Always check their credit rating before you do. Contact other local suppliers—stationery shops, printers, etc.—they do business with and ask them if they pay their bills on time. In fact, frequent buyers may actually ask you if they can open a house account to make it easier to buy from you. Just as customers want to facilitate billing and develop a strong business relationship with you. A house account may also help them to impress their friends and family, which will then undoubtedly result in more business for you.

Any way you decide to extend credit to customers, it's important that you do offer it in some form. As a society, we have a love-hate relationship with credit; but since we do rely on it, you should do everything possible to arrange for acceptance privileges before your first day of business.

Improving Cash Flow

Even though the antiques business is one where the cash flow will be highly erratic at times, you can, to some extent, predict when your cash flow will slow down and when it will be high. This will help you to see which months you should stockpile some of your excess cash in order to provide you with cash flow and income in the down times.

Cash flow is defined as the pattern of movement of cash in and out of a business: revenue and expenses. If you apply for a loan with a bank or other financial company after your business is up and running, you'll have to provide an analysis of your cash flow; if you're just starting out, you may be required to provide the loan officer with a projected cash flow statement.

Cash flow includes all actual monies coming in and going out of the business—cash, checks, and income from credit cards. Depreciation of your office equipment, fixtures, or building does *not* factor into your cash flow analysis.

The first step to improving your cash flow is to increase your revenue so that it is steadier year-round. But despite your best efforts, you'll still have busy and slow periods. There are some things you can do to even out your cash flow a little more.

One way to do this is by attending more proven shows instead of newer ones, holding special sales at your shop, and marketing your business more aggressively during those times of the year when your cash flow needs a boost.

Another way to even out your expenses and therefore improve your cash flow is to ask your utility companies to average out your payments so that you basically pay the same amount each month year-round. And as I suggested earlier, if you stash away 20 percent of your gross revenue during the busy times, you'll have money to draw on during the slow months.

Spotlight

Paperweights

Do you remember that uneven lump of clay that you covered with paint, fired in a kiln, and gave to your mother on her birthday when you were eight years old?

No doubt she treasured it, but not half as much as you'll treasure the appreciation you'll earn if you start collecting unusual and rare paperweights from French and American manufacturers of the 19th century.

Paperweights have always been considered to be more of an art form than a strictly utilitarian object. The talented glass artists who created the paperweights fetching thousands of dollars today used them to showcase their skills.

The popularity of paperweights began to take off in the early 1990s and, several years later, collectors were seeing the prices of their collection double and triple in the course of one year. As of this writing, there are no less than five associations of paperweight collectors; most of these groups publish a regular newsletter and hold periodic meetings.

Although French and early American glass paperweights are most in demand, Chinese and Italian weights, as they're frequently referred to, are also commanding high prices.

Some of the more popular paperweights have flowers or bugs trapped inside them. But whether or not the weight contains an object, its quality—and therefore its value—will be judged by the absence of air bubbles, hairline cracks, and cloudiness.

In 1994, an auction house sold an antique French paperweight from around 1850 for $17,600. The record, set in 1983, was $143,000 for an antique French weight. Most, however, range between $1,000 and $3,000.

Action Guidelines

✔ Subtract your projected expenses from the totals for your estimated gross revenues to determine your expected profit or loss for the year.

✔ Work with your suppliers to develop a credit history that's based on your antiques business and *not* your own personal credit rating.

✔ Select a financial source to help you through the slow seasons, whether it's a line of credit, a business partner, or some money that you've saved from peak times.

✔ Contact credit card companies and make arrangements to accept charge cards from your customers.

GROWTH

Growing a business today can be a challenge. Though everything you will do as the owner of your antiques business will in some way influence how your business grows, most of the time your thoughts will not be on growth, but on putting out all of the little fires that pop up each day. If you have any time or energy left at the end of the day to think about growth, it may be along the lines of how to slow it down so that you'll have at least 15 minutes each day to call your own.

Seriously, growth—or the lack of it—is an issue that every antiques business owner has to face at one time or another. This last chapter will show you how to deal with the variety of ways that growth will manifest itself in your antiques business. And if you've gotten this far in your determination to start your antiques business, handling growth will probably turn out to be the least of your troubles.

The Problems of Business Growth

Many antiques entrepreneurs feel that of all the business problems to have, the kind that involve growth are among the easiest to handle. This is not always so, however. Though by definition, growth means increased revenue and more business, it also means more work and expenses, as well as more headaches.

Some antiques business owners will prefer to grow their business at a slow and steady rate of 8 to 10 percent a year. Others will double their business in one year after they become known for carrying a particular item that's popular. Which is better? While some prefer slow growth so they can learn about the business and grow into it, others say that rapid or sudden growth provides them with a real education of what running an antiques business is all about. It can also provide a much-needed boost to the business when the owner might have otherwise been hesitant about forging ahead. This kick in the pants is sometimes exactly what the owner of an antiques business needs to see it as a business and not just a hobby as is often the case.

Growth *can* be managed and controlled to some extent. How you do it and whether you do it is up to you.

You have some control in the ability to choose to some extent the kinds of customers you wish to have. You can accomplish this by selecting a certain type of antique or collectible to sell as well as choosing the tone of your antiques business. The items you'll sell at auction, for instance, will differ in type and price depending upon whether you sell it through a country auctioneer or an urban auction house like Sotheby's.

One issue you'll face when your business starts to take off is whether or not to hire employees to handle the extra business, or, if you already have help, your decision is going to be whether you should increase their hours to full-time or hire more workers.

You will undoubtedly treat your antiques business as though it were your baby and if you're used to doing it all yourself, you may find it hard to delegate some of the responsibility to someone else, even if it means more free time for you to do other things. Most antiques business owners find that they have difficulty letting go at first. But with time, you will begin to trust in your employees more, which will allow you to give your attention to other problems in the business.

Another byproduct of growth is deciding what to do with the extra money. I can hear you already, "Tough problem to have." Well, once you consider all of your options, you may find that deciding between them will be somewhat difficult. Some antiques business owners use it to pay off some of their personal debts, but the IRS will count these monies as personal income. It's best to pay off debts over time, though some people feel that the savings in debt interest will more than offset the increased tax that you'll have to pay by declaring the money as personal income.

Some antiques entrepreneurs use the extra money to pay off business debts, such as start-up loans. Though it may feel good to own your business free and clear, the deductible interest from your loan payment can come in handy in keeping your taxes down, especially since your business will likely show a larger profit with increased income.

One method that many antiques business owners use to invest the extra money and keep their profits and therefore their taxes down at the same time is to invest more money in the business, whether in capital improvements or inventory. These improvements will enhance your business, attracting even more customers to your antiques. This, in turn, will provide you with more money for even more capital improvements and antiques and collectibles for your inventory for the next year. Of course, as I explained in Chapter 6, you will have to show a profit three out of five years if you're operating as a sole proprietorship or partnership; but if you've been growing steadily, this will not be a problem.

How to Solve Business Problems

Every day that you're running your antiques business, you will undoubtedly encounter a number of problems. Some, will be relatively easy to fix. For others, however, you'll need some help, whether in the form of paid services or good advice from other antique entrepreneurs who have been through it all already.

With some problems, whether they're major or minor, you'll be so busy that you won't have time to think about your options. You'll dig right in then and there and do whatever it takes to get the job done.

If you start to establish a good relationship with other antiques business owners in your geographic area as well as your specialty, you'll have an extensive network of experienced people to call on when you need some answers. Expect also that they will turn to you at some point in the future for your advice and help as well.

Other business owners probably won't be able to help you out with everything, however. On some issues, your local or regional chamber of commerce, antiques dealers associations, and tourist boards will be of help when your problem concerns more specific kinds of advice like what will be the busiest weekends in your area, the best local antiques shows to attend, and which area businesses would like to cooperate on specific promotions.

You'll probably discover that many of the men and women who you already do business with are ideal people to help you solve the problems unique to your business. For instance, your accountant can help you determine how one capital improvement to your business and the projected income it will bring will affect the taxes you'll have to pay next year. So that you can get another perspective, it's a good idea to ask another antiques business owner in your area how business changed after a similar renovation.

Your banker can also help you find answers to your business problems, as well as your lawyer, your real estate agent, and other business owners in your town. In fact, just when you think that there's no one you can turn to for help for your business, you'll discover a surfeit of people ready and willing to help you—and, most of the time, the advice will be free.

No matter what kind of brick wall you're going to hit in the course of running your antiques business, rest assured that you will be able to find help.

Managing Employees for Efficiency

The art of management once prescribed that the boss or manager rule with an iron grip in one hand and a whip in the other. Just like any strict disciplinarian parents and children, both employer and employee were clear who was in charge. The employee went along with this facade, but more often than not managed to get away with things whenever possible and did only what was expected and never anything more.

The opposite philosophy was that of the sensitive manager. He soft-pedaled harsh news, coddled his employees, and always was ready to heap lavish praise at the smallest accomplishment. Again, employees went along with it but felt they were never fully trusted or appreciated for their own talents and efforts. As before, quality and morale suffered.

The ideal management style for a small business is to let employees feel as though they are responsible for the business's success or failure. That is, they should feel like they can treat the business as though it were their own. This, of course, comes not only with a number of perks but also some pretty heavy responsibilities.

This management style is perfect for antiques business owners who need to delegate. It's also ideal because employees in small businesses usually quickly develop a personal relationship with the boss. The type of management that's required to accomplish this balance may run counter to the perceptions that many people think being a boss involves; but in the end, you'll find that your employees will be happier, more productive, and will stay with you longer if you learn to hand the reins over.

It's not so easy, however. People who feel that they have to control their employees in order to get them to work may run into problems with executing this altered style of management. If you fall into this category, once you see that your employees will treat your business almost as well as you do, you'll eventually become a proponent of this management style and actually begin to adapt it in other areas of your life.

Here's how to do it. Say you've just hired a woman to work 20 hours a week at your antiques business, helping out wherever you happen to need it. The both of you should first determine the tasks where she excels and those better left to you.

Initiate a training period where you lead her through the various tasks she'll need to learn, from the way you want the phone answered to the method of selling you prefer: the hard or the soft. Let her watch you perform each task a few times, and then let her do it herself. Assure her that she can approach you with any questions she has, no matter how trivial it may seem. It's important to encourage open communication at all times. Your end of the deal is to remain open to her queries and always respond in a patient, guiding manner.

When it appears she has mastered several tasks, send a few others her way. When she makes a mistake, you should call it to her attention immediately and then, patiently and without judgment, explain to her the way to do it that's best for your business and *why*. Make sure that you're not calling her on the carpet just because she's doing the tasks a bit differently from how you would. In fact, for maximum efficiency, it's a good idea not to get too caught up with how certain things get done, rather, make sure they *do* get done. If you insist that your employees follow particular steps just because that's the way that you do it, you may find that you'll spend time trying to squeeze a lot of round pegs into square holes. The outcome may be the same, but the morale of your employees will suffer, as will the efficiency of your business along with your sales.

As the responsibilities of your employee grow, you may want to increase her pay, based on performance, and give regular bonuses as well as the occasional day off with pay. The idea is for her to feel personally responsible for the happiness of your customers so that you have time to work on your projects.

The secret to successfully managing employees is to show them what to do, trust that they'll do it, and then leave them alone. Though many employees will be taken aback by this unique approach and some will find it to be too alien for their tastes, the great majority will meet the challenge and help build your business while cultivating a strong personal relationship with you.

Some antique entrepreneurs are absolute perfectionists, however, and they think that no one but they know how to do things the right way. Unfortunately, this kind of a manager will find it hard to keep employees and may be burned out by the end of the first year, enduring a constant turnover in staff.

Even with this hands-off management style, you'll still be calling the shots; compromise and acceptance is the name of the game if you want to help your antiques business along the road to steady growth.

Business Alliances

As already suggested, it's a great idea to join the local chamber of commerce, tourism board, or antiques dealers association so that you can meet some of your colleagues. In far too many cases, business owners will look upon other businesses as competition—even if they're in an unrelated field.

But joining forces with other businesses—antiques businesses and others—can more than double your marketing efforts and scope, and result in increased business for all concerned. If you join the chamber of commerce or antiques dealers association, you can meet other people with similar goals: to increase the number of customers. And if you associate with others in different businesses—like an inn, local tour guide, or even a candy shop—you can band together and offer package deals. Because you're both spending time and money to market the package, not only will you reach different groups of people, but you'll also both reach some of the same people twice. Study after study has shown that people usually don't respond to an offer the first time they hear about it. If potential customers hear about your package twice in two different venues, they'll be more likely to inquire about the package, or at least remember it for the future.

But the most valuable part of forming alliances with other businesses is that you'll receive feedback, ideas, and advice from other business owners with a different perspective on doing business in your area. They may run their businesses in a totally opposite way than you do. At first, your reaction may be to scoff at ideas that are so different from yours. But keep an open mind as you listen to what worked for them and what didn't. As you listen, think about how you could apply the same techniques to your business or alter them to fit the idiosyncracies of the antiques business. Even if you paid a consultant big bucks for ideas on how to run your business better, they're still the perspective and ideas of just one person. It's far better to consider many ideas before discarding some than to rely too heavily on one from the outset, and then fail.

If a local antiques dealers association doesn't already exist, it would be to your advantage to form one. This is perhaps the best example of the kind of business alliance you could belong to. The benefits for most organizations formed this way are twofold: first, you have an instant group of peers who are intimately familiar with what you're doing and who can tell you about their own experiences. Second, joining forces with other antiques business owners allows you to market each business more effectively because each is also being marketed as part of an entity. When you form your own association, the first thing you should do is assemble a brochure that lists the name of the association on the cover and describes all of the members inside and what distinguishes them from one another; i.e., one may specialize in Victorian antiques while another may focus on vintage clothing. Include a name, address, and phone number for each; some associations print a local map and plot out each member's location on it. Members can then distribute the brochure in their own shops and through the normal channels of the chamber of commerce, tourist board, and by mail. One of the members typically serves as the main contact for the group, is listed in group ads and write-ups, and may refer callers to other members. I've seen some antiques dealer's associations get a separate telephone number, which they rotate each day or week among the members through the technological wonder of call forwarding.

Again, not only can the association serve as a coalition that combines the marketing strengths of all the members—after all, every member will market its business in a slightly different way—but if a tourist or show visitor picks up your brochure, then sees your name listed in the local antiques dealers association brochure, that's additional exposure for you and another chance at recognition and sales.

Your business alliances and associations don't necessarily have to be with other antiques businesses, however. Hooking up with other businesses whose aims are similar to yours is bound to help everyone's bottom line.

Secrets of Success

In my opinion, the number one key to success in the antiques business is marketing. In this instance, I use the term quite broadly: not only encompassing all the traditional channels, like advertising and publicity, but also your personal public relations campaign or how you interact with customers and prospects.

During every minute that a potential customer is browsing in your shop or booth, you should be marketing yourself, your merchandise, and your business. I'm not talking about the hard sell; after all, you've already got them there in front of you. The secret of success is to get your customers first to buy something, then to return, and finally to tell their friends about the wonderful experience they had spending money with you. This means that you have to constantly be aware of your customers' needs, but without being overbearing. There are customers who will naturally shy away from you. However, most will welcome your personal interaction and service, benefits that are sorely lacking in American retail businesses today. For those who like to be left alone, you have to let the ambiance of your shop and the quality of your antiques and collectibles do your marketing for you. It's usually impossible to predict what kind of interaction customers welcome when they first walk in the door. But as you begin to immerse yourself in the day-to-day operations of running an antiques business, you can't help but learn a lot about people in a very short period of time. Some characteristics you won't like or necessarily approve of, but it's all part of running an antiques business.

You should remember that your marketing job never ends and that goes for both kinds of marketing: through the media, and when your customers are your captive audience, even if you only have their attention for a minute. If you cease to market with either method, you and your business will begin to fade from memory. After all, with the thousands of messages bombarding your customers each day, you'll need to do something to stand out in order to succeed. But that doesn't mean a constant hard sell, either.

So whether a customer buys after seeing an ad or stumbles upon your shop or booth and thereafter becomes a regular patron, you must always be thinking about marketing.

This secret, plus the happiness you'll have because you're running your own business, are the keys to your success in the antiques business.

When To Quit

Burn-out is the number one reason why antiques business owners decide to sell or close down their businesses. It's so very easy to become caught up in your business—from dealing with customers to constantly searching for new items for your patrons—that you soon begin to crowd out the possibility for anything else to exist in your life besides the business. This is especially a problem with antiques entrepreneurs who don't like to delegate tasks and end up doing everything themselves, even if they do have employees.

The second reason why antiques business owners decide to get out of the business is closely tied in with reason number one: running a successful business—or an unsuccessful one, for that matter—is a lot more difficult than it appears on the surface. They underestimate the amount of work and overestimate the amount of money the business will generate—especially the money that will be available for their personal use.

Because of this unrealistic view of the business, people tend to quit the business long before they originally planned. Some

---

You'll know it's time to quit when:

- You no longer become excited about working with a new customer
- The thrill of the hunt for the elusive antique or collectible has faded away
- You decide to cut back on the number of shows you want to do or always send somebody else in your place
- You can't remember the last time you woke up feeling refreshed
- You're so exhausted from overworking that you've lost your enthusiasm for most things

stay in the business for a few years before getting the feeling that it's time to move on to something else. However, some will even leave within a few short months of getting into the business, when they begin to see that not every item they sell will provide the windfall they expected after reading about the record prices in the trade papers. Remember, there's a lot of junk out there and the antiques and collectibles that are written up in the newspapers and magazines are rare exceptions, never the rule.

Of course, there are many antiques business owners who still love the business but who may feel one or all of these symptoms at one time or another. However, the secret to knowing when to quit or cut back is when you feel like moving on and the disadvantages of running an antiques business clearly outweigh the advantages.

You may decide to totally leave the business and in fact, may sell your business to a novice who is leaving his city ways and job behind for the thrill of being their own boss in a dream business. ("Remember when we were that enthusiastic?" you might say.) But many antiques business owners who leave the business actually end up taking a brief hiatus and jump right back in a few years later.

So listen carefully—once you get started in the business of buying and selling antiques and collectibles for a living, you may not be able to stop.

Spotlight

Decoys

Decoys come in wood, plastic, and cork and decoy afi-
cionados swear that some of the more detailed examples
of decoys look so lifelike that if you stare at them long
enough, you'll be able to see them move.

There are a number of decoy shows scattered around
the country each year; naturally, most are held in the
springtime. Like most popular antiques and collectibles,
the value of a decoy depends on its condition, its detail,
and the mark or signature of a prominent decoy artist.
The vast majority of decoys are ducks, but geese, fish,
and even eels are favored by avid collectors; in fact, anything that would attract an unsuspecting mallard or
drake to swim within a range of a hunter's crosshairs
would attract attention by collectors.

At a recent show in New York in 1994, decoys bore
asking prices of $100 to $6,000. Most, however, were
between $400 and $600. Most decoys of good quality
and value that are in demand and sell regularly to collectors were made between the mid-1800s and the early
1900s.

Today, modern decoys are made of plastic. Decoy collectors also favor bird callers—naturally—and other
carved items. In recent years, decoys have been a popular
folk-art collectible, though the average decoy collector—
who tends to be a male in his fifties who treats hunting
and fishing as a religion—would blanch at the though of
a decoy carved in 1915 by a certain Sven Linberg of
North Wildwood, New Jersey, being used as a mantel
ornament.

Decoys attract the most attention—and therefore, the
most money—on the East Coast and in the Great Lakes
states.

Action Guidelines

✔ Be prepared not to like every aspect of growth.

✔ Build a network of supportive colleagues and business professionals you can rely on when necessary.

✔ Learn to manage employees with a hands-off attitude.

✔ Work with other antiques business owners to increase business for all of you.

✔ Keep in mind that marketing your antiques business is a nonstop venture.

✔ Keep your perspective on your life by taking regular breaks from the business.

Appendix
A

Sample Business
Plan

In The Past Antiques Shop

Main Street
Henniker, New Hampshire 03242
603-555-6543

A Business Plan by Anne and Michael Teake

(1)

Statement of Purpose

This business plan will serve as an operational guide and general policy manual for In The Past, a proposed antiques shop to be operated in Henniker, New Hampshire.

Anne and Michael Teake want to borrow $50,000 for the purpose of opening an antiques shop called In The Past, on Main Street in Henniker, New Hampshire. Half of these funds, $25,000, will go toward the initial renovation, initial marketing costs, and rental deposits for the vacant storefront. The remaining $25,000 will go toward securing inventory for the shop. The principals are also investing $25,000, the value of antiques they own and will place for sale in the shop.

(1)

Table of Contents

(1)

SECTION ONE: THE BUSINESS

A. Description of Business

In The Past Antiques Shop will be a 1,500 square-foot antiques shop that caters to both locals and tourists. The town of Henniker is home to New England College, which provides a steady stream of transients into the town year-round. Most items in the shop will range in price from $5 to $200, with 10 percent of the inventory priced above that.

At present, the desired storefront at 111 Main Street has been vacant for six months, since an unsuccessful thrift store closed its doors after two years of business.

To supplement walk-in business, the Teakes will market the shop to year-round residents by offering a search service for any antique or collectible in demand. In order to market the business beyond the immediate area, however, the Teakes plan to attend several shows in the Northeast each year and place ads in the major trade publications.

The Teakes also will provide appraisal and consulting services to customers who seek their expertise from a combined 35 years of serious collecting.

(1)

B. Description of Market

The primary market for In The Past will be local residents—particularly professors and administrators at the college—who have large discretionary incomes, stately old houses, and an appetite for collecting.

A secondary market will be tourists, parents of students, and visitors who will stop by In The Past whenever they're in town to see what's new.

In The Past will pursue its primary market with ads in local newspapers, special promotions, and sidewalk displays in good weather. For the secondary market, In The Past will place brochures in the lobbies of local lodging establishments.

The Teakes goal is to become an antiques service, and not just a shop, for its customers.

(2)

C. Description of Location

In The Past will be located on the Main Street of Henniker, a town with a population of 3,500 and approximately 50,000 transients who visit over the course of a year. Foot traffic will be heavy, as the Golden Seal Restaurant is right next door. After lunch, many diners will feel compelled to browse next door at In The Past.

The storefront is structurally sound with all fixtures intact, but it needs some serious cleaning and decorative touches to make it suitable for the type of antiques shop In The Past will be. The owners will need a variety of tables and showcases to display merchandise in its best light, and they also plan to place room dividers, wall hooks, and window displays in the shop to enhance the atmosphere and entice customers.

(3)

D. Description of Competition

Currently, there is one other antiques business in town, but the proprietor primarily operates it as a search service, and he also does a few shows each year. He accepts no walk-in traffic.

Twenty-five miles away is New Hampshire's famed Antiques Alley, which runs on Route 4 from Chichester through to Portsmouth. Here, there are more than 200 antiques business spread out over a 20-mile stretch of highway. However, these businesses do not pose a threat to In The Past's business, since Antiques Alley is on the other side of Interstate 93, which forms a natural dividing line for the tourist areas of the state. East of I-93, in southern New Hampshire, the attraction is the seacoast, ten miles from Northwood, the geographic center of Antiques Alley. Henniker, on the west side of I-93, is for tourists who prefer unspoiled countryside, lakes, and mountains. There is a lot less competition among the antiques business west of I-93 than for those on Antiques Alley.

(4)

E. Description of Management

Michael Teake has been an avid collector of antiques for more than 20 years and has even exhibited some of his collection at a small number of shows. He is eligible to retire from his job as marketing manager at IMB Products in six months and intends to have everything in place so he will be able to walk into the management of In The Past and have the shop up and running within a month of his last day at IMB.

Anne Teake has worked in the hospitality business on and off during her 25-year career. She took some time off to raise the couple's children and occasionally helped Michael out at various antiques shows. Anne has an extensive collection of Blue Willow china, which was handed down to her from her mother, an inveterate collector. The china will serve as the integrating theme at the shop.

Michael will be in charge of marketing and managing the office, while Anne will handle sales and searches. She will spend two to three days on the road each week looking for inventory for the shop. Both will be responsible for fixing up and decorating the space.

The Teakes have retained the services of both an attorney and an accountant to help set up the business. They intend to join the local chamber of commerce, state and national antiques dealers associations, and the tourism board in order to network with colleagues and learn about businesses in their area.

(5)

F. Description of Personnel

In the beginning, In The Past will hire one part-time employee, a local high school student, to serve customers on Saturday and Sunday. He or she will be paid $5.50 an hour to start, with no benefits. We anticipate this job to consist of 10 to 12 hours a week. In slow times, this position will be either cut down or eliminated.

We don't anticipate the need for additional employees in the near future.

(6)

G. Application and Expected Effect of Loan or Investment

The $50,000 will be used as follows:

Renovations	$25,000
Working capital	15,000
Cash reserve	10,000
Total:	**$ 50,000**

The $15,000 of working capital will allow In the Past to pay the associated costs of starting our business, joining trade associations, subscribing to industry newsletters, and meeting initial expenses. The cash reserve fund will help sustain the business through the slow times, when our expenses remain constant but revenue dips drastically.

We've arranged with the Henniker Bank for a special reserve line of credit of $25,000 to be used for special acquisitions and fees for shows that we hadn't anticipated.

We will also invest $25,000 equity in the form of antiques and collectibles to sell at the shop and through the mail to provide us with additional capital.

(7)

H. Summary

In The Past will be a country-style antiques shop where the emphasis is on affordable antiques and collectibles. The informal setting and decor of In The Past will encourage browsing and several informational displays will teach customers about the previous uses of different kinds of antiques. These displays will change each month.

There will always be a demand for quality antiques in Henniker. Many of the visitors to the area come from more developed areas and are enchanted by the idea of owning objects from the good old days of a supposedly simpler past. In the Past will put these objects within easy reach. The combination of Michael's marketing savvy and Carol's discerning eye will ensure the increased and continued success of In The Past Antiques Shop.

(8)

SECTION TWO: FINANCIAL DATA

A. Description of Sources and Applications of Funding

In The Past Antiques Shop

Sources
1. Business loan	$25,000
2. Line of credit	25,000
3. New investment from the Teakes	25,000
Total:	**$75,000**

Applications
1. Renovations	25,000
2. Working capital	15,000
3. Cash reserve for contingencies	10,000

To be secured by the assets of the business and personal guarantees of the principals, Anne and Michael Teake

(9)

B. Income Projections by Month, Year One

	Jan	Feb	Mar	Apr	May	Jun	Jul	Aug	Sept	Oct	Nov	Dec	Total
Sales	$2,100	$3,200	$2,500	$1,575	$1,800	$3,000	$4,200	$4,200	$3,700	$4,000	$1,700	$2,500	$34,475
Total Sales	$2,100	$3,200	$2,500	$1,575	$1,800	$3,000	$4,200	$4,200	$3,700	$4,000	$1,700	$2,500	$34,475
Operating Expenses													
Mortgage	$775	$775	$775	$775	$775	$775	$775	$775	$775	$775	$775	$775	9300
Insurance	$100	$100	$100	$100	$100	$100	$100	$100	$100	$100	$100	$100	1200
Utilities	$300	$350	$275	$250	$200	$200	$200	$200	$225	$325	$350	$350	3225
Office Supplies	$25	$25	$25	$25	$25	$25	$25	$25	$25	$25	$25	$25	300
Telephone	$115	$115	$115	$115	$115	$115	$115	$115	$115	$115	$115	$115	1380
Credit card commissions	$81	$90	$85	$50	$60	$105	$145	$145	$125	$135	$55	$85	1161
Postage	$50	$50	$50	$50	$50	$50	$50	$50	$50	$50	$50	$50	600
Marketing & Advertising	$125	$125	$125	$125	$125	$125	$125	$125	$125	$125	$125	$125	1500
Legal & accounting fees	$100	$100	$100	$100	$100	$100	$100	$100	$100	$100	$100	$100	1200
Miscellaneous	$40	$40	$40	$40	$40	$40	$40	$40	$40	$40	$40	$40	480
Total Operating Expenses	1711	1770	1690	1630	1590	1635	1675	1675	1680	1790	1735	1945	20526
Net Profit (Loss) Pre-Tax	$209	$1,175	$605	($210)	$55	$1,125	$2,230	$2,230	$1,765	$1,935	($165)	$555	$11,509

(10)

SAMPLE MARKETING PLAN

The Country Peddler Antiques Shop

Tanya is the owner of The Country Peddler Antiques Shop and has been running the business for two years with her husband, Dick. Most of the marketing budget for the shop has gone for advertising in several antiques newspapers and the weekly newspaper. Tanya and Dick are unhappy with the results of the ads. Drawing up an annual marketing plan allowed them to revamp their strategy and anticipate certain times of the year that would require more time and money.

Their allotted budget of $2,500 for the year—5 percent of the shop's gross revenue of $50,000—comes out to about $210 a month. But the months that require more marketing, and therefore more expenditures, are reflected in the chart.

Note: Keep in mind that this is how one business does it. Use this format, but tailor your own marketing expectations and budget to the timetable.

1995 MARKETING PLAN FOR THE COUNTRY PEDDLER

Goals

- To decrease reliance on advertising and create promotions that attract attention.
- To spread out marketing tasks between Tanya and Dick.
- To spend a total of 10 hours a week combined on marketing.
- To bring in more tourist traffic.

Month	Media	Execution	Budget
January	Direct Marketing: Prepare to send price list to house list in March, when business tends to slow down.	Tanya	400 past customers & 600 prospective customers Postage: 1,000 x .29 = $290 Stationery: $150 Total: $500
	Advertising: One weekly newspaper ad	Dick	4 x $30 = $120
	Publicity: Send press release to local papers and magazines about March sale.	Dick	Postage: $10
February	Direct Marketing: Send brochures and price list to prospective customers	Tanya	120 x .29 = $34.80

Month	Media	Execution	Budget
	Advertising: One weekly newspaper ad	Dick	4 x $30 = $120
	Publicity: None		
March	Direct Marketing: None		
	Advertising: Magazines send letters soliciting advertising in summer issues, Dick passes		
	Publicity: Week of March 15th: Send announcements of special summer program to antiques magazines & newspapers, announcing a weekly evening lecture series where we'll host a variety of experts who will each talk on a different aspect of collecting	Dick	$75 for postage and stationery
April	Direct Marketing: Arrange to rent mailing list of tourists from chamber of commerce. Send letter & brochure for summer series	Tanya	$70 for list rental Postage: 700 x .29 = $203
	Advertising: None		
	Publicity: Week of April 1st: Make follow-up calls to editors who received the March mailing about the summer series	Dick	$40 (estimated)
May	Direct Marketing: None		
	Advertising: None		
	Publicity: None		

Month	Media	Execution	Budget
June (busy season)	Direct Marketing: None		
	Advertising: Weekly newspaper ad	Dick	4 x $30=$120
	Publicity: None		
July	Direct Marketing: None		
	Advertising: Weekly newspaper ad	Dick	4 x $30 = $120
	Publicity: Send press kit to national magazines about this year's Christmas open house activities, with photos from last year's events	Tanya	$80
August	Direct Marketing: None		
	Advertising: Weekly newspaper ad	Dick	4 x $30 = $120
	Publicity: Follow-up calls from July's publicity mailing	Tanya	$40 phone bill (estimated)
September (busy month)	Direct Marketing: None		
	Advertising: Weekly newspaper ad	Dick	4 x $30 = $120
	Take out ad in winter issue of regional magazine	Dick	$230
	Publicity: None		
	Other: Start planning Christmas week activities with other businesses	Tanya	

Month	Media	Execution	Budget
October	Direct Marketing: Letter to house list for Christmas open house	Tanya	500 x .29 = $145 Stationery: $75
November (slowest month)	Direct Marketing: None		
	Advertising: Leaf through solicitations for tourism magazines & directories to be published in spring. Take out 1/6 page ad in regional tourism publication	Dick	$230
December	Direct Marketing: None		
	Advertising: Weekly newspaper ad for Christmas activities	Dick	4 x $30 = $120
	Publicity: Call editors to confirm if they'll attend Christmas week activities	Tanya	$40 (estimated)
	Other: Plan Christmas week and help other area businesses with their promotions		Total: $2,942.80

RESOURCES FOR SMALL BUSINESS

Upstart Publishing Company, Inc. These publications on proven management techniques for small businesses are available from Upstart Publishing Company, Inc., 12 Portland St., Dover, NH 03820. For a free current catalog, call (800) 235-8866 outside New Hampshire, or (603) 749-5071.

The Business Planning Guide, 6th edition, 1992, David H. Bangs, Jr. and Upstart Publishing Company, Inc. A manual that helps you write a business plan and financing proposal tailored to your business, your goals, and your resources. Includes worksheets and checklists. (Softcover, 208 pp., $19.95)

The Market Planning Guide, 4th edition, 1994, David H. Bangs, Jr. and Upstart Publishing Company, Inc. A manual to help small-business owners put together a goal-oriented, resource-based marketing plan with action steps, benchmarks, and time lines. Includes worksheets and checklists to make implementation and review easier. (Softcover, 180 pp., $19.95)

The Cash Flow Control Guide, 1990, David H. Bangs, Jr. and Upstart Publishing Company, Inc. A manual to help small-business owners solve their number one financial problem. Includes worksheets and checklists. (Softcover, 88 pp., $14.95)

The Personnel Planning Guide, 1988, David H. Bangs, Jr. and Upstart Publishing Company, Inc. A 176-page manual outlining practical, proven personnel management techniques, including hiring, managing, evaluating, and compensating personnel. Includes worksheets and checklists. (Softcover, 176 pp., $19.95)

The Start Up Guide: A One-Year Plan for Entrepreneurs, 2nd edition, 1994, David H. Bangs, Jr. and Upstart Publishing Company,

Inc. This book utilizes the same step-by-step, no-jargon method as *The Business Planning Guide*, to help even those with no business training through the process of beginning a successful business. (Softcover, 176 pp., $19.95)

Managing By the Numbers: Financial Essentials for the Growing Business, 1992, David H. Bangs, Jr. and Upstart Publishing Company, Inc. Straightforward techniques for getting the maximum return with a minimum of detail in your business's financial management. (Softcover, 160 pp., $19.95.)

Building Wealth, 1992, David H. Bangs, Jr. and the editors of *Common Sense*. A collection of tested techniques designed to help you plan your personal finances and how to plan your business finances to benefit you, your family, and employees. (Softcover, 168 pp., $19.95)

Buy the Right Business—At the Right Price, 1990, Brian Knight and the Associates of Country Business, Inc. Many people who would like to be in business for themselves think strictly of starting a business. In some cases, buying a going concern may be preferable—and just as affordable. (Softcover, 152 pp., $18.95)

Borrowing for Your Business, 1991, George M. Dawson. This is a book for borrowers and about lenders. Includes detailed guidelines on how to select a bank and a banker, how to answer the lender's seven most important questions, how your banker looks at a loan and how to get a loan renewed. (Hardcover, 160 pp., $19.95)

Can This Partnership Be Saved?, 1992, Peter Wylie and Mardy Grothe. The authors offer solutions and hope for problems between key people in business. (Softcover, 272 pp., $19.95)

Cases in Small Business Management, 1994, John Edward de Young. A compilation of intriguing and useful case studies in typical small business problems. (Softcover, 258 pp., $24.95)

The Complete Guide to Selling Your Business, 1992, Paul Sperry and Beatrice Mitchell. A step-by-step guide through the entire process from how to determine when the time is right to sell to negotiating the final terms. (Hardcover, 160 pp., $21.95)

The Complete Selling System, 1991, Pete Frye. This book can help any manager or salesperson, even those with no experience, find the solutions to some of the most common dilemmas in managing sales. (Hardcover, 192 pp., $21.95)

Creating Customers, 1992, David H. Bangs, Jr. and the editors of *Common Sense*. A book for business owners and managers who want a step-by-step approach to selling and promoting. Techniques include inexpensive market research, pricing your goods and services, and writing a usable marketing plan. (Softcover, 176 pp., $19.95)

The Entrepreneur's Guide to Going Public, 1994, James B. Arkebauer with Ron Schultz. A comprehensive and useful book on a subject that is the ultimate dream of most entrepreneurs—making an initial public offering (IPO). (Softcover, 368 pp., $19.95)

Export Profits, 1992, Jack S. Wolf. This book shows how to find the right foreign markets for your product, cut through the red tape, minimize currency risks, and find the experts who can help. (Softcover, 304 pp., $19.95)

Financial Troubleshooting, 1992, David H. Bangs, Jr. and the editors of *Common Sense*. This book helps the owner/ manger use basic diagnostic methods to monitor the health of the business and solve problems before damage occurs. (Softcover, 192 pp., $19.95)

Financial Essentials for Small Business Success, 1994, Joseph Tabet and Jeffrey Slater. Designed to show readers where to get the information they need and how planning and recordkeeping will enhance the health of any small business. (Softcover, 272 pp., $19.95)

From Kitchen to Market, 1992, Stephen Hall. A practical approach to turning culinary skills into a profitable business. (Softcover, 208 pp., $24.95)

The Home-Based Entrepreneur, 1993, Linda Pinson and Jerry Jinnett. A step-by-step guide to all the issues surrounding starting a home-based business. Issues such as zoning, labor laws, and licensing are discussed and forms are provided to get you on your way. (Softcover, 192 pp. $19.95)

Keeping the Books, 1993, Linda Pinson and Jerry Jinnett. Basic business recordkeeping both explained and illustrated. Designed to give you a clear understanding of small business accounting by taking you step-by-step through general records, development of financial statements, tax reporting, scheduling, and financial statement analysis. (Softcover, 208 pp., $19.95)

The Language of Small Business, 1994, Carl O. Trautmann. A clear, concise dictionary of small business terms for students and small business owners. (Softcover, 416 pp., $19.95)

Marketing Your Invention, 1992, Thomas Mosley. This book dispels the myths and clearly communicates what inventors need to know to successfully bring their inventions to market. (Softcover, 232 pp., $19.95)

100 Best Retirement Businesses, 1994, Lisa Angowski Rogak with David H. Bangs, Jr. A one-of-a-kind book bringing retirees the inside information on the most interesting and most lucrative businesses for them. (Softcover, 416 pp., $15.95)

The Small Business Computer Book, 1993, Robert Moskowitz. This book does not recommend particular systems, but rather provides readers with a way to think about these choices and make the right decisions for their businesses. (Softcover, 190 pp., $19.95)

Start Your Own Business for $1,000 or Less, 1994, Will Davis. Shows readers how to get started in the "mini-business" of their dreams with less than $1,000. (Softcover, 280 pp., $17.95)

Steps to Small Business Start-Up, 1993, Linda Pinson and Jerry Jinnett. A step-by-step guide for starting and succeeding with a small or home-based business. Takes you through the mechanics of business start-up and gives an overview of information on such topics as copyrights, trademarks, legal structures, recordkeeping, and marketing. (Softcover, 256 pp., $19.95)

Target Marketing for the Small Business, 1993, Linda Pinson and Jerry Jinnett. A comprehensive guide to marketing your business. This book not only shows you how to reach your customers, it also gives you a wealth of information on how to research that market through the use of library resources, questionnaires, demographics, etc. (Softcover, 176 pp., $19.95)

On Your Own: A Woman's Guide to Starting Your Own Business, 2nd edition, 1993, Laurie Zuckerman. *On Your Own* is for women who want hands-on, practical information about starting and running their own business. It deals honestly with issues like finding time for your business when you're also the primary care provider, societal biases against women, and credit discrimination. (Softcover, 320 pp., $19.95)

Problem Employees, 1991, Dr. Peter Wylie and Dr. Mardy Grothe. Provides managers and supervisors with a simple, practical, and straightforward approach to help all employees, especially problem employees, significantly improve their work performance. (Softcover, 272 pp., $22.95)

Problems and Solutions in Small Business Management, 1994, The Editors of *Forum,* the journal of the Association of Small Business Development Centers. A collection of case studies selected from the pages of *Forum* magazine. (Softcover, 200 pp., $21.95)

The Restaurant Planning Guide, 1992, Peter Rainsford and David H. Bangs, Jr. This book takes the practical techniques of *The Business Planning Guide* and combines it with the expertise of Peter Rainsford, a restaurateur and professor at the Cornell School of Hotel Administration. Topics include: establishing menu prices, staffing and scheduling, controlling costs, and niche marketing. (Softcover, 176 pp., $19.95)

Successful Retailing, 2nd edition, 1993, Paula Wardell. Provides hands-on help for those who want to start or expand their retail business. Sections include: strategic planning, marketing and market research, and inventory control. (Softcover, 176 pp., $19.95)

The Upstart Guide to Owning and Managing a Bar or Tavern, 1994, Roy Alonzo. Provides essential information on planning, making the initial investment, financial management, and marketing a bar or tavern. (Softcover, 250 pp., $15.95)

The Upstart Guide to Owning and Managing a Bed & Breakfast, 1994, Lisa Angowski Rogak. Provides information on choosing the best location, licensing, and what really goes on behind the scenes. (Softcover, 250 pp., $15.95)

The Upstart Guide to Owning and Managing a Desktop Publishing Service, 1994, Dan Ramsey. How to take advantage of desktop computer equipment and turn it into a thriving business. (Softcover, 250 pp., $15.95)

The Upstart Guide to Owning and Managing a Resume Service, 1994, Dan Ramsey. Shows how any reader can turn personnel, writing and computer skills into a lucrative resume-writing business. (Softcover, 250 pp., $15.95)

The Woman Entrepreneur, 1992, Linda Pinson and Jerry Jinnett. Thirty-three successful women business owners share their practical ideas for success and their sources for inspiration. (Softcover, 244 pp., $14.00)

Other Available Titles

The Complete Guide to Business Agreements, 1993, Ted Nicholas, Enterprise • Dearborn. Contains 127 of the most commonly needed business agreements. (Loose-leaf binder, $69.95)

The Complete Small Business Legal Guide, 1993, Robert Friedman, Enterprise • Dearborn. Provides the hands-on help you need to start a business, maintain all necessary records, properly hire and fire employees, and deal with the many changes a business goes through. (Softcover, $69.95)

Forecasting Sales and Planning Profits: A No-Nonsense Guide for Growing a Business, 1986, Kenneth E. Marino, Probus Publishing Co. Concise and easily applied forecasting system based on an analysis of market potential and sale requirements, which helps establish the basis for financial statements in your business plan. Book is currently out of print, check second-hand bookstores for the title.

Guerrilla Marketing: Secrets for Making Big Profits from Your Small Business, 1984, J. Conrad Levinson, Houghton-Mifflin. A classic tool kit for small businesses. (Hardcover, 226 pp., $14.95)

How to Form Your Own Corporation Without a Lawyer for Under $75.00, 1992, Ted Nicholas, Enterprise • Dearborn. A good book for helping you to discover all the unique advantages of incorporating while at the same time learning how quick, easy, and inexpensive the process can be. (Softcover, $19.95)

Marketing Sourcebook for Small Business, 1989, Jeffrey P. Davidson, John Wylie Publishing. A good introductory book for small business owners with excellent definitions of important marketing terms and concepts. (Hardcover, 325 pp., $24.95)

The Small Business Survival Kit: 101 Troubleshooting Tips for Success, 1993, John Ventura, Enterprise • Dearborn. Offers compassionate insight into the emotional side of financial difficulties as well as a nuts and bolts consideration of options for the small businessperson experiencing tough times. (Softcover, $19.95)

INDEX

A

Accountants, 106-107

Accounting, 120-121; software, 37-40

Action guidelines, 20, 42, 74, 93, 109, 127, 146, 161, 176

Advertising, 78, 85-88 ; on a budget, 136-138; in trade publications, 7. *See also* Marketing

Advice, solicitation of, 32, 166, 170

American Society of Appraisers, The, 66

Announcements, 95

Answering machine, 37, 81

Antique, definition of, 11-13

Antiques business, envisioning yours, 77, 80-81

Appraisal services, 3, 10-12, 50, 65-66

Apprenticeships, 34

Assets & liabilities, 36-37

Associations, trade, 34, 47, 130

Attitude requirements, 35-36

Attorneys, 105-106, 166

Auctioneers, 10-11; profiles of, 21-22

Auctions, as marketing tool, 22; proliferation of, 11-12

B

Banker, 166

Book shop, used, 110-111

Bookkeeping. *See* Accounting

Books, 6-7, 34; for antiques business, 57-59; four-color, 11; for small business, 197-203

Booksellers, antique, 58-59

Borrowing money, 154-156

Bridal registry, 143

Brochures, 7, 33, 78, 130, 133, 140-142

Business, alliances, 169-171; cards, 33; description, 181; name, 33, 80, 98-99; types, 102-105; your place in, 2-11

Business plan, sample of, 177-190; writing of, 78, 81-84

Buying a business, 89-91, 114

C

Capital, 156-157

Cash, accounting, 120; flow, improving, 159

Chamber of commerce, 98, 130, 144, 169

Classified ads, 143

Coins through mail order, 6-7

Collectors Net on-line system, 39, 40

Company Memorabilia, 108; Hoosier Cabinets, 19; Lenci Dolls, 41; Paperweights, 160; Pez Dispensers, 145; stock and bond certificates, 92

Standards, maintaining, 35-36

Start-up, 97-111; costs, 33; from scratch, 87, 89, 114

State Antique Dealers Associations, 50, 98

Statement of Purpose, 179

Stationery, 33

Step-on guides, 144

Success, opportunities for, 1-22; planning for, 77-96; requirements for, 23-45; secrets of, 171-172

Suppliers, antique, as resource, 34, 47, 50; antique, attitude toward, 35-36; of display equipment, 63-65; working with, 154

T

Taxes, 124-125. *See also* IRS

Technology, 37-40

Testing your business idea, 97-98

Time management, 135

Title search, 106

Tools & Equipment, 30-32

Tourist trade, 143-144, 170

Trade, associations, 50-55, 169-171; publications, 6, 11, 15, 34, 47, 60-63; placing ad in, 33, 85

Training, job, 10, 47, 55-56

Travel, love of, 8-10

U

Unpredictability of antiques business, 2

Untraditional markets, 142-144

V

Venues, variety of, 2-3

W

Warranty deed, 106

Where to Sell it, 9

"Who-buys-what books," 9

Windows software, 37-38

Word processing software, 37-40

Workshops. *See* Training, Seminars

Y

Yard sale finds, 15-16

Z

Zoning, 102